A Seeker's Theology

Christianity Reinterpreted

Mystical Faith for Skeptical Christians

Revised Edition

**A Retired Episcopal Priest,
Now a Quaker,
Discusses: Mysticism,
God, Jesus, Doctrine
Bibliolatry, Panentheism,
The Religious Society of Friends**

John G. Macort

ISBN: 13: 978-1540500724
10: 1540500721
Printed in the United States

<u>Note</u>: Much of this book was taken from lectures delivered previously by the author. Readers may notice great amounts of repetition in the text. These were included in order to use each section as a separate lecture. Since not everyone was present for every lecture, much information was repeated. It also enables each section to be read as a self-contained unit.

Contents

Contents (continued)

(Much of the text was transcribed from previous lectures.)

Preview

God is not a supreme being or divine person, not a super-human in a mythological "heaven" separate from earth. That "God" does not direct the affairs of humanity, or move mankind around like toys, determining our fate. That "God" does not exist.

Fundamentalism is a tragic and devastating misunderstanding of Christianity.

Most of the narratives in scripture are not historically true, as we define "truth" today. They are legends, myths, parables, poetry and hyperbole.

There were no Adam and Eve. There was no fall from grace. There was no original sin.

Jesus was not born in Bethlehem. He had a human father and mother. He was born in Nazareth.

Jesus's death was not a sacrifice to pay for sin.

Jesus's corpse did not rise physically from a tomb. Jesus was, and is, experienced alive, appearing mystically in various forms as a glorified body.

The terminologies of the three Christian creeds and of orthodox doctrines are confusing and more misleading than helpful. They presuppose an anthropomorphic God in "heaven." This is pure Olympian mythology. Revise it! It distorts Christianity.

What theological reasons caused early Quakers to reject Catholicism, Calvinism and Anglicanism? I agree with each of their theological reasons, even if they are deemed to be heretical by most Christians.

God is a power within everything that exists, within every person, every object, and yet beyond all of existence. God is eternal "Existence" itself. Quakers refer to God as the "Inner Light." The man Jesus, was a unique human manifestation of God. Many other persons manifest God also. God is in everyone. God is in all things, everywhere. God can be experienced, but never defined.

Scripture and Christian doctrine can be understood only through a mentality completely different from our normal perceptions. This is the mystical realm of the numinous. It is a level of consciousness through which we experience God and all the great figures of Hebrew and Christian history. They evoked an overwhelming sense of awe that could be explained only through legends, myths and hyperbole. When meditating upon legends, we see beyond them, through "direct revelation," mystically experiencing those great figures, personally and alive.

God can be experienced through meditation into a mystical realm. For me, this is best found in Quaker Meetings. In silence, God within us comes to Light. We find direction and power to go into the world to work for peace, justice, equality and the right of every person to live in the very best ways possible for all of humanity. God is in every person, the Inner Light. That is why I now identify with the Religious Society of Friends.

The Author's Context:
Episcopal-Skeptic-Seeker-Quaker

This book describes my life-long journey to an identity with the Religious Society of Friends (Quakers.) I am a retired Episcopal priest, who has served four parishes as associate rector and rector. During that time, I also taught Theology, Church History, Moral Theology and Philosophy in a Roman Catholic preparatory school, a Roman Catholic university and at various other colleges. During my frustrating search for religious identity, I have lived as an Anglo-Catholic, a "liberal" Episcopal priest, briefly as a Roman Catholic layman, with life-long Quaker influence. Throughout those years, I was searching for mystical experiences, which happened for me mainly among Quakers, or in other secular situations. In this book, I focus on the theological reasons why the early Quakers rejected Catholicism, Calvinism and the Church of England. I agree with those theological reasons, along with many other reasons why I identify with Quakers. Many Quakers do not discuss theology, certainly not in Meetings. I believe that it is important to explain some basic Quaker theological beliefs, why they originally developed, and how they differ from other Christian theological concepts.

From early childhood, I attended a Quaker school, a Quaker college and had family ties to Quakerism. During those years, I attended Thursday Quaker Meetings every week of the school year, and often on Sundays with my parents or friends. Since my retirement on any Sunday morning I often have attended an early Eucharist at a local Episcopal parish, and later gone to the nearby Friends Meeting. Sometimes, I attended a Roman Catholic Mass, a Unitarian lecture, or a Buddhist meditation. God is in every person, every aspect of creation, every faith, everywhere! I reject religious or denominational boundaries.

For extended times during the past years that I was active as a priest and teacher, my faith constantly was challenged. Finally, it left me with nothing but doubts. For many years, I was an agnostic, even while celebrating the Eucharist and preaching in some parishes to well over a thousand parishioners every Sunday. Later, I realized that my agnosticism was the result of my traditional, orthodox theology. That has changed.

As a child, I had attended a very "High" Episcopal or Anglo-Catholic parish. I loved all the ceremonial, the processions, the chants, incense, the "smells and bells." Like many Christians, I thought of God as the divine being or

8

celestial person, who controlled every part of human life. God, therefore, was the cause of both good and evil experiences. My childhood picture of God was an old man in the heavens (with a long white beard, of course.) If I prayed fervently enough to that God, perhaps my prayers would be answered. I was told by a Sunday school teacher that God saw everything that we did. She told the class that God had a huge book with everyone's name in it throughout the world. If we said or did something bad, God would put a black mark by our names. When we died, we would go to heaven or hell depending on the number of black marks that we had accumulated. How could this God keep track of the billions of people on earth every second? I suppose today my teacher would have to tell the class that God had a huge computer! She scared the hell out of most of us children. That concept of God had driven me to non-theism and agnosticism.

The old questions of theodicy haunted me. How can a benevolent God allow such horrible suffering? Why do good people suffer and evil people prosper? Where is justice? God had to be imagined and experienced differently! How does one do that, when scripture, creeds, doctrines, liturgies, sermons and prayers all seem to portray God as my childhood images?

Initially, with most Christians, I believed that Jesus was God incarnate, the eternally existent "God the Son," who "came down from heaven," as stated in the creeds. He was sacrificed on a cross to appease the wrath of God the Father, making possible the forgiveness of the sins of mankind. That conjured up thoughts of an angry, jealous, anthropomorphic God with human emotions, who was bent on punishing people. A horrible myth! I reject that concept of "God," along with all of its theological implications.

Over the years, I realized that most of scripture consists of mythology, metaphors, parables and legends. I never was a Biblical literalist or fundamentalist. Still, my faith rested upon a "traditional" idea of God that I could not accept rationally. Most of my faith collapsed into cynicism and rejection of much of Christianity. For a while I thought that I still could believe the Christian creeds symbolically. Now, I believe that the symbols themselves are very misleading. The terminology needs to be changed. How?

Orthodox Christian doctrines still assume an anthropomorphic God somewhere in a place called "up in heaven," separate from humanity. The three creeds of the Christian Church seem to "dissect" Jesus, attempting to prove how he could be both human and divine. They all sound to me like ancient Greek, Olympian mythology.

Jesus was fully human, a man who lived his life as a unique, human manifestation of God. To know the man Jesus is to know God. I rest my faith on that belief, and need no further theological explanations. Jesus is the image of the unseen God. ("Colossians" 1:15.) Jesus was a man who could love absolutely. God is love. Therefore, Jesus is the image of God. That sums up my faith. I experience God within myself, in all persons and in all existence. That is what Quakers call the "Inner Light" and "direct revelation." It is a mystical experience, not in scripture or doctrine.

I experience Jesus through his direct revelation, mystically, in a different realm of consciousness. I identify with the words of the Right Rev'd. John Shelby Spong: "I seek a Jesus beyond scripture, beyond doctrines, beyond dogmas and even beyond religion itself. Only there will our gaze turn toward the mystery of God." [1]

In spite of my otherwise liberal theology, I always have retained an appreciation for the Eucharist. I still believe that it is a mystery, a gift, but experienced only through the lens of mysticism. In the Eucharist, Christ mystically becomes present. I believe that the Eucharist is a joining of the human and the divine. Mystical is more profound than symbolic, metaphorical or metaphysical. Mystical consciousness is the lens to faith. Sadly, in recent years, I have not found the mystical experience in the Eucharist that I once encountered and cherished. For decades, I have searched for it in Anglican and Roman Catholic celebrations. A necessary atmosphere of mystery and solemnity seems to have been lost. The words of the liturgy express a theology that I cannot accept. Prayer is not begging a far-off "God" to come "down to earth" and magically fulfill our wishes. I believe that prayer transmits the energy of love to other persons.

Theology, as most Christians know it, must be reinterpreted with different terminology and metaphors. Liturgies must be rewritten with completely different language and symbols. The old faith has to die before the new faith can live! That is a challenge that most clergy are afraid to confront. Whenever I delivered a sermon, and referred to certain scriptural readings, I always told my congregations that this account is considered by most Biblical scholars to be a legend, myth or parable. Then I would ask what it means for us today. Not every parishioner agreed with my critical approach to scripture!

12

So often, people who are skeptical about Christianity ask me how I can believe all of that "stuff" that Christians believe. My short answer is, "I do not." The literalistic concepts that most people have of Christianity have kept thousands out of churches. They are unbelievable. We can experience a sense of awe with new awakenings from reading scripture as metaphors, parables, and legends. Literalism offers some people a false sense of religious certainty and security. It turns others away from the Christian faith. It deprives them of the wonderful treasure of experiencing God through mystical, direct revelation. I believe that God is found within ourselves, within every other person, and in all that exists, not in scriptural literalism or in doctrines or creeds.

My responses to these challenges of faith have led me to the belief that the path for me, personally, is to follow the practice of disciplined meditation. Through meditation one mystically can enter a completely different realm of under-standing. This has been called the "realm of the numinous," (Rudolf Otto.) It is a total rejection of literalism. The legends and parables of scripture point beyond themselves to greater truth that cannot otherwise be expressed. I believe that we must delve beneath the legends and myths to discover what originally had inspired people to create them, to pass them on orally, and later, in writing. Who were those original persons who evoked such overwhelming awe that created the bases for the myths and legends? I believe that we can get to know and experience those giants of our Hebrew-Christian heritage through personal, direct revelation within the realm of the numinous, a level of consciousness often called mysticism.

The mysticism of the Quakers, and that of many other religious experiences, all stem from a numinous level of consciousness. Quaker meditation brings us to an overwhelming sense of awe and divine presence. Through those mysteries, we experience God. These experiences may happen in many ways. Certainly, I have felt the same awe and presence of God through nature, music, friends and family. The Religious Society of Friends is a total way of life that not only sustains my faith, both emotionally and rationally, but it offers me the power and presence of God to put my faith into action in the service of mankind. I have returned to my early roots among Quakers. Finally, I feel at peace with myself, with God, with those around me, with my "liberal," anti-discrimination and anti-war political activism, with my worship, volunteer services, and with my faith.

John G. Macort, B.A., M.ED., M.DIV., M.A. REL.

14

You do not have to believe
what you always were taught.
There are other ways of
thinking,
            interpreting,
                        believing:
Another consciousness.

The Realm of Faith, Mysticism,
the Sacred and Spiritual.

The Numinous Realm

Forget the mentality of reason
and provable perceptions.

Enter a Different Dimension.

The Realm of the "Numinous"

All my discussions about the problems of interpreting scripture and doctrines literally or historically have led me to some conclusions that differ radically from traditional, orthodox Christian theology. I approach these revelations in terms of "the sacred numinous realm" and "mysticism."

The theologian Rudolf Otto used the word "numinous" to express what is experienced in religious consciousness as the "holy." It expresses feelings of overwhelming awe in the presence of a power both from within and also beyond. Otto used the Latin term *Mysterium Tremendum.* (The Idea of the Holy.) [2] It says to the divine, "Thou art in me and I am in Thee." There exists a "numinous realm" of consciousness. It is very different from our normal mentality. "Numinous" comes from the Latin word *numin,* which refers to divine power, spirit, evincing the deity. It means sacred or holy, separate from the mundane. It creates an arousal of religious emotions which are otherworldly, mysterious, mystical and awe inspiring, surpassing comprehension. It refers to being in the presence of the divine.

Whenever we ponder scripture or doctrine, whenever we imagine or invoke God, whenever we think about Jesus, we must put ourselves in the realm of the numinous. That means blotting out any context of literalism, metaphysics, science, history or truth as we define these in terms of contemporary consciousness. It means putting ourselves into another realm, a spiritual realm, the realm of those who first experienced Jesus and his Hebrew ancestors. It is the realm of the saints, the mystics who believe that they have experienced a personal and real presence of God and of the living Jesus Christ. Most minds of modern western culture are not "geared" to make such changes in their mental frames of reference.

The writers of scripture took stories of great people in Hebrew history that had been passed on orally from their original sources. Those original source persons had known and experienced those people and events personally, firsthand. Their stories were written decades or centuries later. Those original source persons must have had overwhelming, inspiring experiences that could not be explained in matter-of-fact terms. The only ways that their emotional, awe-struck experiences could be expressed was through great exaggerations, myths and legends. Those original source persons had experiences in the realm of the

17

numinous. What they encountered was beyond all realities of this physical world that we all live in and know. Their experiences were mystical, mysterious, supernatural and beyond any description. They were in a different dimension, beyond this world, yet they were very real. The same can be said for those who knew and followed Jesus. We can know Jesus through the "lens" of the numinous, mystical realm. This awareness is called by Quakers, "direct revelation."

The sacred realm of the numinous is found within ourselves. God is within us. If we probe the depths of our consciousness, we can leave behind our usual ways of thinking, and reach a spiritual dimension beyond our contemporary frames of reference. That context is a different mode of thinking, feeling and believing. It is the realm of faith. It is experiential. Although the narratives in scripture are not what we normally would call true or historic, they usually were created to point to meanings beyond themselves. We do not ask if something actually happened or is historically true. That is the wrong question. It is real on a very different level of consciousness. Jesus is revealed as the manifestation of God. God exists within us. Meditation is the path to that direct revelation and faith. That is mystical.

Mysticism

Mysticism cannot be defined. Like so many other concepts associated with religion, it must be experienced. I use the term very loosely. Some would relate the term to a state of ecstasy. I am using it in a different and much wider sense, which does not necessarily reach any form of ecstasy. A broad and always insufficient explanation of mysticism might suggest that it is a sense of becoming at one with God. God permeates a person's experience. For some, it may refer to the attainment of insight into sacred beliefs. It refers to an altered state of consciousness. It involves delving into our real selves, what we consider to be most basic in ourselves and in our lives, and there, discovering God. Mysticism is found in most all religions, from primitive to highly organized ones. It is common in various forms of Catholicism, Eastern Orthodoxy, Celtic Christianity, Buddhism, (Zen,) Judaism, Taoism, yoga, Hinduism, Islam (Sufism,) among Druids, Native Americans and in various other forms of meditations. God is experienced in many ways.

In his book, <u>Understanding Mysticism,</u> Richard Woods, O.P. begins with a chapter by Margaret T. Smith. I quote Margaret Smith:

Mysticism is not to be regarded as a religion in itself, but rather as the most vital element in all true religions, rising up in revolt against cold formality and religious torpor. Nor is it a philosophical system, though it has its own doctrine of the scheme of things. It is to be described rather as an attitude of mind; an innate tendency of the human soul, which seeks to transcend reason, and to attain a direct experience of God. Mystics believe that it is possible for the human soul to be united with Ultimate Reality, when God ceases to be an object, and becomes an experience. Mysticism has been defined as the immediate feeling of unity with God. It is the religious life at its heart and center.... The self and the world are forgotten. The subject knows himself to possess the highest and fullest truth. [3]

Margaret Smith continued, saying that the aim of mystics is to establish a conscious relation with the Absolute, in which they find the personal object of love.[4] That spiritual union is the presence of God in all creation and in love.

Margaret Smith stated that mysticism postulates certain assumptions. It believes that mankind can receive direct revelation and knowledge of God. It believes also that the human self can know "Reality," and that every creature, by nature, is akin to God. "There is within every living soul a divine spark, that which seeks reunion with the Eternal Flame. The mystics throughout the ages have contended that God is 'the ground of the soul,' and that all men in the depths of their being, have a share in one central, divine life." [5] (Richard O. Woods, O.P.)

I do not claim to be a mystic. I am stating only that the way that I attempt to understand scripture and the Christian faith is by assuming that much of the content has been expressed as responses to mystical experiences by the authors of the books of scripture. By assuming that the authors of scripture were basing their writings on their personal mystical experiences, that is "direct revelation," I can understand why they wrote as they did. It is impossible to express in words what one experiences mystically. The scriptures were not written to convey historical, factual truth. The creators of each narrative used legends, myths and exaggerations to try to express what otherwise could not be articulated. As we read scripture, we need to ask the questions, "What over-whelming and unique experiences of awe were the sources of these legends and metaphors? What was revealed to them through their experiences?" Something very real caused those responses! We must translate those experiences into a numinous realm, and assume that the writers (speakers) were expressing themselves in mystical terminology. Then, through focused meditation, we can share, mystically, some of those original experiences.

I believe that Jesus Christ was a true mystic, as were many of the authors of the books of scripture. The same may be said about the saints and myriads of devout Christians. Mysticism is a personal and direct awareness of the presence of God. It is an experience which seems to enlighten a person's understanding of spiritual dimensions. Somehow, it brings a person into that dimension, as if enveloped by a presence of the divine. It is a step far beyond myths, legends and symbols, into an awareness of where those symbols attempt to lead us. It is an awakening beyond normal consciousness. It is a very personal experience of overwhelming awe which cannot be described.

Rufus Jones, the famous Quaker philosopher, saw mysticism as the basis of Quakerism.[6] A mystical experience enlightens a person to an awareness of the presence of God within the self, and within all others. "Thou art in me, and I am in Thee." We know this personally, he claimed.

Regular, disciplined meditation is the pathway to the experience of mysticism. I try to meditate regularly, especially in Quaker Meeting. At times, I have experienced a presence, a power, a serenity from beyond me, which then becomes part of me. This has happened during a Catholic (Anglican or Roman) Mass, or on the beautiful mountain where I grew up, or by the sea where I have spent most of my adult life. It can be awakened by music, or inspired by experiences that create an overwhelming sense of awe, amazement, identity with my surroundings, or with other people. Identity with other people is called "love." These are times of enlightenment, insight into hidden truths, of great emotional responses and a sense of awe. Mysticism can lead one into the sacred, spiritual, numinous realm.

Numerous examples of mystical experiences appear in the scriptures. Certainly, Moses had a mystical vision of God while on Mt. Sinai. Moses was said to have glowed with the radiance of the Spirit. When he returned, in spite of their disobedience, his followers renewed their faith in his leadership. Ezekiel envisioned the heavenly throne of God and a chariot of fire. Elijah was believed to have been transported to heaven in a chariot of fire. (Chariots and thrones were common symbols in Hebrew mysticism.)

Jesus climbed up a high mountain with Peter, James and John. He was so much at one with God, that, like Moses, he was transfigured. He glowed with the intense Light of the divine. ("The Transfiguration," Matt. 17:1-8, Mark 9:2-8, and Luke 9:28-36. See pages 151 and 152.)

Those who encountered Jesus as alive after his crucifixion all were overwhelmed by mystical experiences of his presence with them. For them, Jesus was as present with them just as really as he had been before he was crucified.

Saint Paul, then "Saul," had a mystical experience on the Damascus road. It was as if "scales fell from his eyes." Suddenly he "saw" and understood. Those experiences were real for each of those persons. They were not hallucinations or dreams or tricks of the imagination. But, they were not perceivable events in the terms that we would define perceptions of something that is actually before us, or can be proven scientifically or historically. They simply become realities through a different mode of consciousness. These were mystical, direct revelations. They inspired extreme reactions. Those indescribable reactions are expressed in terms of hyperbole, symbolism, legends and myths. No rational or literal explanations can suffice.

The Religious Society of Friends

There are many reasons why I still identify with the Quakerism of my youth, and attend Friends Meetings regularly. One reason is Quaker mysticism. An hour of silent meditation enables me to get in touch with myself, my deepest feelings, with the God within me and beyond me, the God in all persons and in all of existence. I have rejected any literal acceptance of scripture and Christian creeds. In Quakerism, there are no creeds or doctrines. Also, as a pacifist, I agree strongly with Quaker efforts for peace and justice for all people. Quakerism is a way of life. Quakers live and act on their beliefs. God is present in every person! These beliefs express my faith.

Although I have been an Episcopalian for most of my life, I attended a Quaker school during most of my elementary and preparatory education, and then went on to a Quaker college. My mother spent much of her childhood living with a Quaker family at the beginning of the last century. I have attended Friends Meetings whenever possible. The Quakers taught me that God is a presence and power in every person. They called it the "Inner Light." The Quakers use the phrase, "holding a person or concern in the Light" to mean offering intercessory prayer for that person or concern.

When Quakers (Friends) first gather for Meeting, they meditate quietly. One becomes aware only of the absolute, weighty silence. First, one must clear his or her mind of all the mundane distractions that need to be addressed. Some may pray for their families and personal concerns. Then, when minds seem clear, it becomes possible to concentrate on allowing that "empty" mind to contemplate whatever seems to be flowing into it. When one reaches that point, it is called "Centering Down." One may focus on an idea, or simply allow ideas to flow freely and undirected. At some point, a person may speak, usually briefly, about his or her thoughts, sharing insights with the others. When this happens, it is said that the person has been "moved by the Spirit" to speak. During any hour-long Meeting, there may be one or three or five or more speakers, or there may be no speakers at all. The silence envelops each person with a sense of the presence and peace of God. Problems fall into a context of serenity and hope. They become illuminated by the Light.

These beliefs lead to a response of caring for others, both near and far. There is an awareness of responsibility to serve others, to reach out in love, and to work generously and actively for the good of all of mankind. It is a response to feeling at one with God, with all of humanity, and with all of creation. An inner serenity then evokes an obligation to bring peace to all the world. Through meditation, Quakers share the hopes, the joys, the fears, the suffering and sorrows of others. Prayer is an expression of love, which then must be turned into actions involving every aspect of life.

Since Quakers believe that God is within every person, moral obligations become clear. Do not harm or kill anyone. Refrain from any form of violence or retaliation. Strive to settle disputes through peaceful and respectful negotiations, and not by force or military power. Protect the environment, the earth. Work to find methods to cure diseases, to reduce hunger and poverty. Practice simplicity in all of life so that others may live.

God's "Light" and common ground can be found among all people. Quakers do not proselytize or try to convert people to their beliefs. They help everyone suffering from war, natural disasters, oppression, discrimination, famine, poverty and disease. Quakers often offer food and medical aid to the enemy as well as to allies. "The temple of God is sacred, and you are that temple." (I Cor. 3:17.) That applies to every human being. Since God is in every person, then the faiths, beliefs, religions and customs of all people must be respected, whether or not they are Christian or think as we do. Who is to say that the Light of God cannot enlighten all religions, as it shines fully in Jesus Christ? God can be experienced through all approaches to religions and faith.

Around the year 1647, the Quaker movement began in England, led by George Fox and others. Since that time, there have been many varieties and expressions of Quakerism. Some of these differences have led to serious divisions. There is great diversity among members of The Religious Society of Friends. I shall not attempt to describe these specific differences as they developed throughout the centuries, but I'll focus on the theological issues that relate to scripture, doctrine, direct revelation, God and Jesus.

The place of Jesus of Nazareth had been central to Quakers from the beginning. Since then, however, there have been differences of opinions about Jesus and his relation to God (Christology.) Some "modernist" Quakers contend that one does not need to be a Christian to be a Quaker. That has created some controversy. Originally, Quakers were very strongly Christian, although they differed on many theological beliefs from most other Christians of their era, such as Catholics, Calvinists, and Anglicans. Quaker roots were Christian, but today there are many varieties of branches. In some Meetings, there seldom is any mention of Jesus. In others, he may be spoken about, but usually with emphasis on his humanity rather than divinity. Each Meeting is unique. (I am more Christocentric than many liberal Quakers.)

From their beginnings, Quakers have looked to scripture for guidance and inspiration, but they were ahead of their time by not interpreting it literally, as did most Christians. Quakers have held to the belief in direct revelation. Scripture is considered to be metaphorical and allegorical, but not literally true. Still, it remains very important, as the foundation of the Christian faith. The Holy Spirit continues to reveal to each individual the essence of faith, just as various expressions of faith were revealed to the writers of scripture.

For most Quakers, "direct revelation" has been the foundation of their faith. It means that through mystical experiences, usually arising from deep, God-centered meditation, one can become aware of the presence of God and the meaning of life as each person confronts daily situations. The Inner Light reveals God's will to each individual directly and personally. The profound, cryptic meanings of scripture and the mysteries of theology can be revealed best through direct revelation.

One of the main controversies within Quakerism was whether scripture or the Inner Light through direct revelation should be primary in understanding one's faith. In 1676, Quaker Robert Barclay wrote in his _Theologiae Verae Christianae Apologia,_ that the central doctrine of Friends is the Inner Light. Direct revelation is superior to scripture. By the end of the eighteenth century, however, Quakers had become seriously divided over the issue. Elias Hicks (1748-1828) rejected the authority of scripture, and stressed direct revelation of the Inner Light. Many of the conservative and evangelical Quakers (Wilburites and Gurneyites) broke away from the followers of Hicks. Today, influenced greatly by philosophers such as Dr. Rufus Jones and my former teacher, Professor Douglas Steere of Haverford College, the mystical nature of Quakerism has become the central focus for most Quakers. Scripture must be illuminated by the Inner Light within every person. Faith, therefore, is inward, personal and subjective, directly revealed to each person, individually, by God.

Previously, Quakers were known for their strict, puritanical prohibitions, typical of nine-teenth century, conservative Protestantism. More recently, however, most prefer moderation to prohibitions. Traditionally, Quakers do not have clergy. Some Meetings, however, especially in the midwestern United States, have programmed services and ministers. Their services are similar to many conservative Protestant services, with scripture readings, hymns, prayers and sermons by a pastor. Many tend to be evangelical, and stress the centrality of scripture. Some may lean toward fundamentalism. Those Quakers are very different from other much more liberal Quakers, many of whom are more Unitarian. Eastern Quakers tend to have traditionally silent worship.

In his booklet, "Speaking as One Friend to Another," John Yungblut, a Quaker, wrote:

> Mystical religion stresses the immanence of God without denying transcendence.[7] All mystical religion involves an inward journey to the self, to the Self and God....[8] God is nearest me and in me. That God is the very Self of myself, and we are all members of one God-body, which is the very ground of our being.[9]

Quakers reject creeds and doctrines. This is expressed in the following quote:

> Religious experience is beyond linguistic codification and definitions. Creedal

31

statements demean, in their limited linguistic form, the depths of religious experience. Creedal statements operate to close off new religious expressions and revelations. Creedal statements encourage a complacency of attitude to religious life by giving an impression of finality and security. Creedal statements take on an authority of their own belying the authority of God. A creedal statement would be impossible, inappropriate and dishonest because of the diversity of individual beliefs. [10]

Because the Inner Light of God is in every person, when Quakers are trying to reach a decision about a controversial issue, or about any business resolution, they do not vote. When a group votes on any matter, some win and others lose. Quakers work, sometimes at great length, through discussions and meditation, to reach a "sense of the Meeting" at any deliberation. They seek agreements that will seem appropriate and fair for everyone concerned. Everyone is equal.

In the past, Quakers have suffered per-secution for their beliefs. They had refused to bow or remove their hats before authorities in England. Because they refused to fight in wars, or join the established denominations, they often were fined, beaten, imprisoned and even executed. They do not swear oaths. They always have worked for civil rights for all, and were strong leaders in the Underground Railroad during the American Civil War. Today, in the United States, Quakers may be granted conscientious objector status. Many who refused to fight, have served as medical staff or in other non-combatant positions. All these tenets are based on the belief that God is in every person. Therefore, every person should be treated as one whom God loves, in spite of how one may feel about those persons, or consider their actions to be harmful or evil. That can be a difficult challenge! It is an ideal, but ideals must begin with those who are willing to try to live by them. That may risk serious conflicts with the rest of society.

Some have criticized Quakerism because of its lack of defined doctrines to pass on to future generations. Quakers have many specific beliefs, such as equal rights for all, non-violence, service to others, aid to the impoverished, to refugees and minorities, support for ecology and conservation. Quakers are known for their simplicity, thrift, honesty and respect for all persons. But, they allow for great variety in matters of faith. They gain faith through divine, direct revelation. They express their faith through actions. Quakerism, more than a religion, is a total way of life. Peace!

Quaker Philosophers:
Rufus Jones and Douglas Steere

When I was a student in 1956 at Haverford College in Pennsylvania (a "bastion" of Quakerism,) Dr. Douglas V. Steere was my professor of philosophy. He often said that the mysticism in Quakerism and that in Roman Catholicism are very similar. He said that Quakerism is the "crown" or "pinnacle" of Catholic mysticism. God is believed to be present through both. Professor Steere often compared many Catholic mystics with Quakerism. Dr. Steere was speaking only about Catholic mysticism, and not about doctrines or common beliefs. He included in this theory also the Catholic Mass or Eucharist, so long as it was understood as a mystical experience.

Douglas Steere based much of his philosophy on that of his predecessor at Haverford College, Dr. Rufus M. Jones. Both Douglas Steere and Rufus Jones had more influence than any others in modern times to emphasize the mystical foundations of Quakerism. For years, I have pondered the theories of Rufus Jones and Douglas Steere. They are among the main themes that inspired me to write this book. The basis of the Christian sacraments is mystical. All of life is a sacrament! Catholic mystics seem to affirm this.

Catholic Mystics and Quakers

"The mysticism that is basic to understanding Quaker beliefs is a direct and parallel continuation of the mystics of the ancient and medieval Catholic Church. Quakers are neither Roman Catholic nor Protestant, but are a unique and separate expression of mysticism that preceded and has influenced both."

Copied from notes taken from lectures by Professor Douglas Steere, Haverford College, Haverford, PA. 1956.

Four steps on the ladder which leads to mystical communion with God are:

Reading scripture
Meditation
Prayer
Contemplation

Guigo II, 12th century monk.

This also is Quakerism!

Quotes from Catholic Mystics

St Augustine of Hippo

St. Augustine (354-430) was consecrated a bishop of Hippo in northern Africa in 395. There, he established a religious community, and became one of the most prominent bishops of the Church. He is known also for his defenses against heretics. His two most popular books are <u>Confessions</u> and <u>City of God</u>. Some of his mystical quotes from his book <u>Confessions</u> are:

"Do you not believe that there is in man a depth so profound as to be hidden even from him in whom it is?"

"The same thing which is now called the Christian religion existed among the ancients. We have begun to call 'Christianity' the true religion which existed long before."

"Faith is to believe what you do not see. The reward of faith is to see what you believe."

"I could not find you, Lord, because I erred in seeking you without, when you are within."

"God is best known in not knowing him."

"When I come to be united to thee with all my being, then there will be no more pain and toil for me, and my life shall be a real thing, wholly filled by thee."

"I will plant my feet on that step where my parents put me as a child, until self-evident truth comes to light."

"It is no advantage to be near the light if the eyes are closed."

"Deity is inscribed on every heart."

"What does love look like? It has the hands to help others. It has the feet to hasten to the poor and needy. It has the eyes to see misery and want. It has the ears to hear the sighs and sorrows of man. That is what love looks like."

(All of these quotes can be found on the internet under "Quotes from St Augustine of Hippo." See also "The Mystical Saints," and "Famous Catholic Mystics.")

Guigo II, "Lectio Divina"

Guigo II was a Carthusian monk. He was prior of Grande Chartreuse monastery from 1174 until 1180. He died in 1193. One of his best-known writings is The Ladder of Monks, subtitled "A Letter on the Contemplative Life." Another is The Twelve Meditations. These are among the first, and certainly very famous descriptions of the four steps that make up the mystical tradition of *Lectio Divina.* He envisioned a ladder that was made of four rungs or steps that lead to closer mystical communion with God. The *Lectio Divina* has served as a basic guide for contemplation in monasteries and convents to this day. It expresses also the same guidelines that Quakers offer for meditation.

1. Reading: Enter a tranquil state of mind in a quiet place with no interruptions. Select a passage of scripture, and read it multiple times.
2. Meditation: Listen for the most profound meanings of the scripture as revealed by God.
3. Prayer: Communicate with God through prayer. Listen for God's message to you.
4. Contemplate: Reflect on that revelation.

(From the internet, Lectio Divina.)

St. Francis of Assisi

St. Francis of Assisi (1181-1226) is one of the most famous and beloved saints. Having been born to wealth, he devoted his life to poverty and concern for the poor. He had many mystical visions of Christ. His faith and life have served as beautiful examples for Quaker beliefs and ways of life.

"We never should desire to be over others. Instead, we ought to be servants who are submissive to every human being for God's sake."

"While you are proclaiming peace with your lips, be careful to have peace in your heart."

"Great and gracious God, and Thou Lord Jesus, I pray thee shed abroad thy light in the darkness of my mind. Be found within me, Lord, so that in all things I may act only in accordance with thy holy will."

"Pure, holy simplicity confounds all the wisdom of this world, the wisdom of the flesh."

(From the internet, "Christianity Today, Quotes: Francis of Assisi.")

St. Teresa of Avila

As I remembered the words of Professor Douglas Steere from his lectures on Quaker philosophy at Haverford College, delivered in 1956, I was relieved to have found some of my notebooks, saved in an old trunk in an attic. They were written during many Haverford classes over 60 years ago. In class, Professor Steere assigned extensive readings from Saint Teresa of Avila's writings, including her <u>Autobiography</u>, <u>Interior Castle</u> and <u>The Way of Perfection</u>.

Saint Teresa (1515-1582) was born in Avila, Spain. She became a Carmelite nun. Throughout her life she suffered from many illnesses. She often experienced visions and heard voices. Some of these might be considered bizarre or even deranged. That is not uncommon in the visions and dreams of some mystics. St. Teresa worked hard to reform the Carmelites, blending a highly active life with deep contemplation. She was declared a Doctor of the Church in 1970 by Pope Paul VI, the first woman to receive that honor.

The following quotations may be found on the internet, "Teresa of Avila - Quotations."

"Let the truth be in your hearts, as it will be if you practice meditation, and you will see what love we are to have for our neighbors."

The Way of Perfection.

"You must not build upon foundations of prayer and contemplation alone, for, unless you strive after the virtues and practice them, you will never grow to be more than dwarfs."

Interior Castle.

"Mental prayer is simply a friendly and frequent conversation with Him, who, as we know, loves us."

The Life of St. Teresa of Avila by Herself."

"Reflect carefully on this, for it is so important that I can hardly lay too much stress on it. Fix your eyes on the Crucified, and nothing else will be of much importance to you."

The Way of Perfection.

"It is quite important to withdraw from all necessary cares and business, as far as is compatible with the duties of one's state of life, in order to enter the second mansion." (Mysticism.)

The Way of Perfection.

St. John of the Cross

St. John of the Cross, (1542-1591) was born Juan de Yepes y Alvarez in Old Castile, Spain. With Teresa of Avila, he established the Discalced Carmelites. He is recognized as one of the greatest mystics of all times. Among his writings are <u>Dark Night of the Soul</u>, <u>Spiritual Canticle</u> and <u>Living Flame of Love</u>.

"Mystical wisdom, which comes through love, need not be understood distinctly…, for it is given according to the mode of faith, through which we love God without understanding God."
(Spiritual Canticle, Prologue #2.)

"In the dark night of the soul, bright flows the river of God."

"This dark night of sense is an inflowing of God into the soul, called infused contemplation or mystical theology. God secretly teaches the soul and instructs it in the perfection of love."
(Dark Night of the Soul, Chapter 5.)

Quotations taken from the internet: "St. John of the Cross, Quotations."

Meister Johannes Eckart

Meister Eckhart (1260-1328) was influential in shaping Christian mysticism during the late Middle Ages. He taught that the goal of a Christian should be union with God. He believed that within every person was a divine spark. Through this spark, one could unite with God. Eckhart entered the Dominican Order and taught in Cologne, Germany. He denied that reason alone could inform any idea about the nature of God. God lacks any form that can be known to mankind. God could be known only through personal and subjective mystical experience. As a forerunner of Paul Tillich, Eckhart declared that God was not "out there" beyond us. God is within every person, and every person can become one with God. He taught that a mystic must reject any finite or humanly proposed ideas about God. He said that our existence must be God's existence, and God's existence must be experienced as our existence. Today, his theology would be called "panentheism." (Page 61.) The authorities of the Church questioned the orthodoxy of many of his ideas. Shortly after Eckhart's death, Pope John XXII condemned most of his writings as heretical. His ideas influenced the early Quakers, George Fox, James Naylor, Robert Barclay and their followers.

Quotations from Meister Eckhart

"We all are meant to be mothers of God…for God is always needing to be born."

"Nobody at any time is cut off from God."

"I need to be silent for a while, words are forming in my heart."

"One must learn an inner solitude, wherever it may be."

"All God wants of a man is a peaceful heart."

"Run into peace."

"The price of inaction is greater than the cost of making a mistake."

"God is at home. It is we who have gone out for a walk."

"What a man takes in by contemplation, that he pours out in love."

"Truly, it is in darkness that one finds light, so when we are in sorrow, then the light is nearest of all to us."

"We must learn to penetrate things and find God there."

"The eye through which I see God is the same eye through which God sees me; my eye and God's eye are one eye, one seeing, one knowing, one love."

"Be willing to be a beginner every single morning. Suddenly you know it is time to start something new, and trust the magic of beginnings."

"I am sure that nothing is so near to me as God. God is nearer to me than I am to myself. My existence depends on the nearness and the presence of God."

"Theologians may quarrel, but mystics of the world speak the same language."

"A human being has so many skins inside, covering the depths of the heart. We know so many things, but we do not know ourselves. Why?"

Quotations are from:
https://www.goodreads.com/author/quotes/
73092Meister_Eckhart

Right Brain, Left Brain

In psychology, there is a theory which is known as the "lateralization of brain functions." It has been held by psychologists Hughlings Jackson, Brenda Milner, Roger W. Sperry and others. It states that the right and left sides of the brain tend to create certain different characteristics. A person who is left brain oriented may tend to be more logical, literalistic, analytical, mathematical, objective, focused on perceptions and scientifically proven facts. A right brain dominated person may tend to be more artistic, musical, creative, subjective, philosophical, emotional, mystical, contemplative and religious. That may be represented more by Eastern thought. Mysticism appeals to the right hemisphere of the brain. This psychological theory often can be exaggerated. Of course, all these characteristics overlap in every person.

I believe that much of Western Christianity has lost the mysticism necessary to understand and appreciate scripture. As the early Christian Church moved west from the Jews to the Greeks and Romans, the Hebrew mind was replaced by the Hellenistic and the Latin mind. Much of the essence of Judaism and early Christianity was no longer understood. The ancient Hebrew mind was

"Eastern" or right brain. It saw life in contemplative, symbolic, mystical terms. It expressed itself in parables, myths and legends. Traditionally, the ancient Eastern mind has defined history and truth differently from the modern "Western" mind. (One cannot explain "Eastern" and "Western" in terms of geography. They refer to modes of thinking. Some of the most profound examples of mysticism are found in Irish Celtic Christianity, the most western land of Europe, and among Native Americans.)

Not only does the left dominated brain desire to understand things more literally, it also is uncomfortable with mystery. It wants answers, facts and proof. The right dominated brain is comfortable with mystery, and tends to explain those mysteries through symbols, the arts and parables. It possesses a sense of mysticism, an awareness of a spiritual world beyond this, a dimension that cannot be known or described without a sense of the holy or the "numinous of religious consciousness." I refer again to Rudolf Otto's concept of *Mysterium Tremendum* in his book <u>The Idea of the Holy</u>. [11] I have found this very profoundly in Quaker meditation and also in some Roman (or Anglican) Catholic experiences of the Eucharist. In some denominations choirs, organs, chanting, candles, incense, bells, statues, stained glass, elaborate vestments and other ceremonial acts add much to produce a solemn atmosphere of the numinous realm. Music can evoke our faith. It can create an emotional mood. Absolute, silent meditation can do the same.

In his book, <u>Sacred Silence,</u> Donald Cozzens quotes Karl Rahner's book <u>Concerns for the Church,</u> saying, "The Christian of the future will be a mystic or he will not exist at all." Cozzens went on to write, "Today's Christian is challenged to bring a contemplative dimension to his or her life." [12] The concept of the numinous realm as an alternative form of consciousness, is basic to this understanding of the Christian faith. It opens the door to "direct revelation" and communion with God. It appeals to the right side of the brain.

In summary, the real question is whether "direct revelation" is a valid concept that actually enables a person to communicate with the divine. Can it "enlighten" people to the will and workings of God? Or is it all an imaginary theory? Is it just one more human attempt to find God? That Is a matter of faith!

The Holy Eucharist
Holy Communion, Mass,
Divine Liturgy
The Eucharist As Mystical

In spite of all of my liberal theology, and
many long periods of agnosticism, the one
constant belief that never has left me has been my
belief in the mystical presence and power of God
in the Eucharist. (Also called the Holy Communion, the Mass, or in Eastern Orthodoxy, the Divine
Liturgy.) Gradually, however, in my later years, I
have come to realize that my beliefs were rooted
in the mystical realm of the numinous, and not in
any rational or doctrinal foundations. The power
and presence of Christ in the Eucharist can be
experienced, but never defined. The Eucharist
must be experienced mystically. For many
Christians, it is the center of faith and worship.

Now I understand why, for the past few
decades, I have been so frustrated when attending
celebrations of the Eucharist in Anglican or
Roman Catholic churches. The solemnity, the
awesome sense of mystery, the emotional arousals
of the past, so necessary for my own experiences
in the Eucharist, all have disappeared in most
churches. The ambiance of absolute silence has

been destroyed by talking among the congregation before and during the celebration. Gregorian chants, incense, bells, all of the "props" traditionally used to create a solemn ambiance seldom are present today. The exchange of the "Peace," which is a prescribed, limited response, has been turned into a time for people to leave their pews, hugging and having long conversations. In some parishes, one even hears applause. None of this lends itself to any kind of mystical experience. The Second Vatican Council was very necessary. But, how can the Church be stripped of superstition and still inspire a sense of mystery and awe, which, for me, evoked a mystical experience.

Another problem that I have had with the Eucharist is very personal and results from having been a priest for many decades. In 1969, I published a book on liturgy and ceremonial for priests. During any celebration of the Eucharist, I find myself engrossed in judging how the priest is celebrating the liturgy, rather than concentrating on the mystical experience of the Eucharist. The old "high" or "low" church divisions return to haunt me. That is my "baggage" from the past that now distracts my personal meditations. The words and ceremonial of the liturgy, even the music, have become distractions instead of aids. Today, I prefer silent meditation.

As will be discussed in future chapters, the symbols and statements in the liturgy presuppose an anthropomorphic God somewhere off in the sky, removed from humanity. The theology that describes this human-like, celestial being is obsolete and unbelievable. All of this has interfered with my experience of the Eucharist. For me, this all must change. But, when and how?

Except for the Eucharist, my personal faith has wavered on almost every other issue of Christianity. During my darkest days as a priest, for long periods of time I could believe almost nothing about Christianity. But, I had to celebrate the Eucharist almost every day. Never! Never, however, did I approach the altar without suddenly believing that I was about to celebrate the transformation of bread and wine into the body and blood of Jesus Christ, the presence of God. My mind might have been in a turmoil of rejection as I read scriptures or listened to a sermon or recited the Nicene Creed. But, the moment that I walked to the altar, genuflected and kissed it, I was a priest of the Holy Catholic Church. This was a Catholic Mass (Anglican,) and Christ was present, physically, as flesh and blood in the host and chalice. During the 1960s, some of my Roman Catholic priest friends used to say, "There is no God, but Mary is his mother." I was saying,

"There is no God, but this is his body and blood." Now I realize that whatever happened each time I celebrated the Eucharist was a mystical transformation of myself and my faith. I entered the sacred, numinous realm. The Eucharist is a mystical experience. It cannot be reduced to definitions. Doctrines can destroy the mystical experience which must remain a personal mystery.

It is impossible to describe or define what the Eucharist is about in rational terms. Still, I shall attempt to offer some explanations as they often are presented. First, it is important to define the concepts of "memorial" or "memory" as a Hebrew in Jesus's day would have understood them. In that Semitic culture, to "remember" an event from the past does not mean merely to recall or to bring it to mind. Through "remembrance," an event from the past, actually becomes as real in the present as it originally was in the past. To "remember," as I believe Jesus used those words during his last supper with his friends, evokes not only the same reality in the present, but also energizes the same power that those words had when he first spoke them. For a Hebrew, words have power. Note that in a "Genesis" myth, the author said that God created the universe through the power of the spoken word. A blessing or curse had powers to bring about certain results. Therefore, at each Eucharist, the act of remembering, called the "anamnesis," brings about the same realities and powers as did Jesus's words spoken on the night before he was handed over to be tortured and crucified. By remembering Jesus's words as they are repeated in the Eucharist, it is believed that the Church has the power to proclaim that the bread and wine on an altar, truly become the body and blood of Jesus, just as he said that they would at that last supper before his crucifixion. That is mystical, and based on faith.

As Jesus offered the bread and wine at that supper, he also announced his forthcoming death. That announcement of his death cannot be separated from his words that the bread and wine were his body and blood. They were what soon would be his tortured, bleeding body on a cross. The power of those words remembered and spoken at each Eucharist, therefore, have the same effectiveness in the present as did Jesus's death on the cross 2000 years ago. For this to be true, the Eucharistic bread and wine mystically become the body and blood of Jesus Christ. This belief is basic to Anglicans, Roman Catholics, Eastern Orthodox and most Lutherans. The Eucharist brings God to us, now, mystically, in the form of a consecrated sacrament, but just as really as Jesus did personally, two millennia ago. The Eucharist is a bridge between God and God's people. This is not a mere symbol. For believers, bread and wine become mystically, Jesus's body and blood.

The Roman Catholic concept of "Transubstantiation" as defined at the Lateran Council in 1215 stated, "The Mass is a real and genuine sacrifice, in essence identical with the sacrifice of the cross, only different in manner." [13] This was the cause of many divisions during the Protestant Reformation. Some misunderstood the Sacrifice of the Mass to mean that Jesus somehow dies repeatedly. This misconception was explained by St. Thomas Aquinas in the words, "different in manner." Very simply stated, Aquinas based his teachings on Platonic dualism. That philosophy maintains that every object has an "essence," that is, what it really is. Every object also has "accidents," meaning the ways in which we perceive it. For instance, an oblong shaped, wooden board may be supported by four posts and be painted brown. The wood, shape, posts and color are the accidents. The essence, what it is, is a table. At the consecration of bread and wine during the Eucharist, the accidents, being bread and wine as we know them, remain the same to our human perceptions. Their essence, however, becomes the actual body and blood of Christ. That is what they become, mystically. Such dualism is foreign to the contemporary Western mind. For me, the Eucharist is a mystical expression of faith, but not doctrinal. It is an experience which cannot be explained in rational or theological terms.

Rather than try to explain the Eucharist in the traditional Semitic, Platonic or Aristotelian terms, I often refer to the explanation given by the sociologist Joseph Campbell, a man whose work I greatly admire. (Joseph Campbell, 1904–1987, was known for his writings and lectures especially in the fields of mythology and comparative religions.) In attempting to explain the mystery of the Eucharist, I look to Joseph Campbell's story of human sacrifice and cannibalism among pre-historic tribes. Campbell explained that the strongest, most virtuous, handsomest, wisest, fiercest warrior and most loved member of a tribe would be sacrificed. His dead body would be eaten, or cremated and the ashes eaten by members of the tribe. In doing so, those who ate a part of this man's body were believed to gain some of his marvelous attributes, his virtue, strength, wisdom and so on. The same is true in the Eucharist. When we eat Christ's body, his attributes, his powers become part of us. This enables us to have faith, to love, to forgive, and to choose to live more virtuous lives than otherwise would be possible for us. Through the Eucharist, we take these attributes, these virtues of Christ into ourselves. Christ became the fulfillment of that universal myth, which was expressed as human sacrifice in primitive cultures. Now we call it "the Sacrifice of the Mass." [14] The myth becomes a real experience. This is mysticism, the realm of the numinous.

Although I still believe that there is an objective, real presence and power of God in the Eucharist, I believe that God must be experienced personally and mystically. Perhaps this all demonstrates the theories of Rufus Jones and Douglas Steere. Quakerism is the "pinnacle" of Catholic mysticism. I believe that the Eucharist can be universalized to include the flesh and blood of millions of others who have been killed for their religious or political beliefs. Consider Socrates, Joan of Arc, William Wallace, Abraham Lincoln, Mohandas Gandhi, Martin Luther King, Jr., John and Robert Kennedy. (For many, this is heresy!) Call me an "Episcopal, Catholic, Quaker." I reject all denominational limitations and identities. Recently, however, my need for the outward and visible signs of any sacrament has diminished. I find the presence of God more directly in the "sacrament of silence" of a Quaker Meeting. That was the experience of the early Quakers. All of life is a sacrament. I have returned to Quakerism.

God

God is not a "divine person" or "supreme being" in "heaven" who governs the fate of humanity like a "celestial puppeteer." That theistic image of God is pure mythology and unbelievable theology.

Anyone who presumes to define God reduces God to man's image. God can be experienced, but not defined. Creeds and doctrines fail.

We experience God as part of us, a "Light" in every person. God is "Existence." We exist as part of all existence. God is "ALL." [15]

Theology cannot be approached in a logical way like algebra. One theory does not always lead to another.

God

My awareness of God exists in the realm of the numinous through mysticism. I do not believe that God can be defined, explained or experienced through the same rational mentality and consciousness that we normally use in most of our thinking processes. Therefore, as I shall discuss later, I have serious doubts about any form of doctrines that attempt to explain, define or dissect God. In this, I identify more with Quaker beliefs than with traditional, orthodox Christian creeds and doctrines. I consider the Nicene Creed to be statements of confusing, obsolete metaphors, not literal truth. Usually, when I attend a Eucharist, I do not recite it. (See page 170.)

I have rejected the commonly held images of God. The God of the ancient Hebrews dwelt in a heavenly dimension in the sky, and intervened into the human world to manipulate the events of every person and activity on earth. That is called a *deus ex machina*. That concept of God, as a divine person is called "theism." The theists' God was created in the image of man. He was a superman-God, who, much like the gods of mythology, had human attributes, but was a divine being. I am not an atheist, neither am I a theist.

(I refer to Paul Tillich's theology.)[16] I am a "non-theist" Christian. (See "Panentheism," page 61.)

The God of the early Hebrews was their heavenly king. He lived on a mountain, but later was believed to be present in the temple in Jerusalem, and in the sky. He was a warrior God, who led the Hebrew people against their enemies. He was male in contrast to many of the female deities of the neighboring cultures. He made covenants with the Hebrew leaders, Abraham, Noah, Moses and others. The Abraham covenant was a promise that he always would be the God of the Hebrews, and they would be his people. The covenant with Moses contained laws of the Torah. There were stipulations in this covenant. God would favor the Hebrews so long as they kept the laws. Otherwise, they could be punished.

This God knew everything that each person did. He had human emotions. He could be jealous and vengeful. He would judge us after our deaths, and had to be appeased by our constant confessions and pleas for mercy. This deity could be swayed by our fervent prayers, and would enter our human realms to control our lives. One could bargain with him as was told in "Genesis" 18:22-33, when Abraham tried to bargain with God to save Sodom. God decided what would happen to each of us, how we would live and when we would die. His anger against us for our sins and the sins of all of humanity had to be appeased by blood offerings. Those offerings could be made by sacrifices, such as the pascal lambs at Passover, or on the Day of Atonement, by the scapegoat (*azazel,*) who took on the sins of the Hebrew people and was driven into the desert. Later, that sacrifice was made by the death of Jesus of Nazareth, who was called God's Son. That implies that this God (the Holy Spirit) somehow was the biological father of Jesus. Still, every person would be judged after death, and be sent to such "places" as heaven, purgatory, or hell. To me, this God, up in heaven, separated from the world, does not exist. It all is a myth that defies human reason. But, it is a concept of a deity that has been, and remains, prevalent among the majority of Christians throughout the ages. It is a theology that I reject. It is God created in man's image.

From this theistic, mythological concept of God came the images of God as "Father." Because we cannot imagine God, and yet we want to have a relationship with God, traditionally people have envisioned God as "Father." This is fine, so long as we realize that God is not a person or being off in heaven. "Father" is a term that we use to address what we cannot imagine or state in words. It is a symbol that points to a mystery. Jesus addressed God as "Father." He even went so far as to call God "Abba," a very familiar term such as "Daddy" or "Papa." This imagery may help people to feel God as Love. Since we may feel the need to picture or imagine God, this traditional and ancient symbol may be helpful to many people as a focus for meditation and prayer. When we visualize God as a divine person, however, we must be aware that we are creating God in our own images. We do not know how Jesus envisioned God (Father) in his mind. I believe, however, that Jesus was at One with God.

Panentheism: God in All, All in God

I believe that God must exist in every person and in every object that exists, and yet God is more than existence. This concept of God is called "panentheism," which means "all-in-God-ism." Perhaps this was what I always believed, but never really could explain. At first it reminded me of the pantheism that I felt as a teenager, when I somehow experienced divinity in the beautiful mountains, the sea, in the animals, the forests, and in my friends and family. Pan**en**theism, however, is not pantheism. (The two letters, "en" make a huge difference.) It goes beyond pantheism to include all of existence, and more than existence.

61

It says that God is within all that exists, but greater than existence, and also apart from existence. God is in every atom, every cell, every star in the cosmos. God is in the energy that creates and sustains all things. God is in evolution. God is eternal Existence itself. [17] God is both immanent and transcendent, that is, within us and beyond us.

God is present in all things, but also beyond and distinct from all things that exist. God is "ALL." God is my existence and the existence of all other existence in infinity and eternity. We all are related as we all share that divine Existence with God. We all are united as "One."

God as "Existence"

In 1962, I spent time in England taking courses at St. Augustine's College in Canterbury. One of my theology professors was the Right Rev'd. John A.T. Robinson, then the Bishop of Woolwich. Later that year, Bishop Robinson published his book, Honest to God, which shook the foundations of Christian theology. Robinson based much of his theology on the works of Dr. Paul Tillich, an extremely famous theologian, who was a Lutheran minister and a professor of theology at universities in Germany. In 1933, Paul Tillich came to the United States, and was appointed professor of philosophical theology at the Union Theological Seminary in New York. Paul Tillich stated that God is the "Ground of All Being." God is "Being" itself, "ultimate reality," the foundation of all that exists.[18]

More recently, my beliefs about God as "Existence" have been inspired by the Episcopal Bishop, John Shelby Spong, in his book, Eternal Life: "A New Vision."[19] Many of Bishop Spong's ideas are based especially on the theology of Dr. Paul Tillich. For these theologians, God is not a person or a being. God is not "out there," removed from the earth. God does not visit the earth, or manipulate all the human events that take place. Because God cannot be imagined, symbols are necessary when discussing the concept of God. But, symbols themselves can be misleading. They create an irrational mythology if taken literally.

Bishop Robinson quoted Paul Tillich's words, "The name of this infinite and inexhaustible depth and ground of all being is 'God.' That depth is what the word 'God' means.... the depth of your life, the source of your being, of your ultimate concern, of what you take seriously beyond any reservation." (Quoted from a collection of Dr. Paul Tillich's sermons entitled, "Shaking of the Foundations.")[20] God is not a supernatural being existing beyond the earth who can intervene from without (perhaps from a place called "heaven") to manipulate the lives of mankind. God is within us. Quoting Paul Tillich again, Bishop Robinson wrote, "For the word 'God' denotes the ultimate depth of all our being, the creative ground and meaning of all our existence." [21]

Many Christians still think of God as a person-like being separate us and from the universe. This is "theism." They speak of "Our Father who art in heaven," a "person," in a "place" beyond the world. This is called "transcendence." Transcendence means that God is beyond us, an entity separate from us.[22] The Bible speaks of a transcendent God and also of an immanent God. "Immanent" refers to God dwelling within us. "Acts" 17:28 says that God is the one "in whom we live and move and have our being." God is both immanent and transcendent. God is beyond us, and also all around us and within each of us. God dwells in everything, and everything dwells within God. This is a definition of panentheism. It is very different from picturing God as "a great old man in the sky," who controls human events on earth. I identify with panentheism. I think of God as a presence and power within me, and in all others, the Inner Light.

A problem arises when people question the existence of God. A person, a being or a thing can cease to exist. If one cannot see or perceive such a being or thing, one can say that it does not exist at all. (I am not talking about microscopic particles or objects out beyond our universe. That is a different issue.) The only thing that one can say truly exists, is "existence" itself. We cannot say that existence does not exist. If we think of God as Existence itself, then God must exist.

The question arises, how did existence first begin? This is not an argument resulting from the question of first creation, or who created the creator. Rather, it maintains that creation itself is of God, and God is within all of creation. God is not separate from creation. God did not exist as a person or being or power beyond creation, who at some event created all that exists. God is more than everything that exists in the universe, the cosmos and beyond. God is not merely the "first cause." If existence is eternal, then God is eternal and *vice versa*. The eternity of "Existence" (God) is an assumption that must be accepted in faith.

In "Exodus" 3, a story is told about how God appeared to Moses in a vision of a burning bush that the fire would not consume. Moses wanted to know God's name. God's answer was, "I AM," or "I AM WHO I AM." The ancient Hebrews recognized that "I AM" referred to God. We find this in the Hebrew scriptures, and also in the fourth gospel. ("St. John.") "I AM" means "I exist." The use of the term "Ground of All Being" (Paul Tillich) means that God is the Existence of all that exists. (Bishop John Shelby Spong.)

The reference to God as "I AM" is very important in the "New Testament" as the gospel writers' indications that Jesus was divine. In the fourth gospel, the author equates Jesus with "I AM." The author refers to each event of the Hebrew liturgical year, and demonstrates how Jesus is the fulfilment of each event or symbol of those events. Jesus is portrayed as saying "I am" to each of these. Jesus says I am the true vine, the light of the world, the gate of the sheepfold, the bread of life, the resurrection and the life, and so on. The author goes on to claim that Jesus said, "Before Abraham ever was, I am." ("St. John" 8:55.) To any Jew of Jesus's time, that would have meant that Jesus was claiming to be divine. (I do not believe that Jesus ever could have said any of those words. See pages162 and 163.)

See pages162 and 163.

God as eternal "Existence" is fully discussed in Bishop John Shelby Spong's book, Eternal Life: "A New Vision."

God as Creator

From the earliest of times, people have wondered who made the earth and sky and sun. Who made us? There must have been a creator. From those questions came various myths and legends about a creator and creation. We find two of these very different myths in "Genesis," chapters one and two, the first having been written much later than the second.

If it is assumed that a supernatural deity, somewhere removed from creation, created all that exists from outside of it, then that deity must not be a part of creation. Therefore, people imagined that God was "in heaven" removed from the earth. Panentheism proposes that God is not separate from creation. God is within all of creation, and all of creation is within God. Yet, God is more than creation. God exists eternally.

God as "Logos:" Wisdom – Word

Closely related to the concept of God as creator, is that of God as wisdom, cosmic intelligence, the "Logos" or "Word." In the "Old Testament," divine wisdom is manifested in creation, and in the divine guidance of individuals and nations to do the "will" of God. ("Proverbs" 8 and "Wisdom" 7:22 ff.) In the "New Testament," divine wisdom is incarnate in Christ, whom Paul calls "the power and wisdom of God." ("First Corinthians" 1:24.) The Holy Spirit also is associated with wisdom, as one of the gifts of the Spirit. In "The Gospel According to St. John," wisdom could be understood as synonymous with the Logos. (Christ.) In Greek, the word *logos* has numerous meanings. Heraclitus (500 B.C.E.) thought of *logos* as universal reason which created and governed everything in the universe. Philo saw it as an intermediary agent between God and the world. In the prologue to the fourth gospel ("St. John,") Logos is equated with God the Son, who existed from before all times (eternally,) and was incarnate in the man, Jesus of Nazareth. ("St. John" 1: 1-14.)

In English, that reference to Logos is translated as "Word," referring to Christ. "In the beginning was the Word, and the Word was with God, and the Word was God…. Through him all things came to be." The gospel goes on to say that the "Word" was the true light who enlightens all mankind. He came into the world that he had made. "The Word was made flesh and lived among us." In the prologue to John's gospel we find an interesting use of the concept of Logos referring to Jesus, and yet *logos* was known by its Greek readers also to mean "wisdom." Today, one might call it "cosmic intelligence." Logos, here, referring to Jesus, is divine wisdom which creates, orders and continues to direct the process of everything that exists. [23] All human intelligence is derived from Logos. It is more than mere knowledge. It is dynamic wisdom which constantly expresses the will of God as it creates. It refers also to Christ.

This theory of Logos creates problems for me. It assumes that God is separate from creation. At some point in time, God the Son (Logos) sojourned on earth as a man, and then returned to a "place" beyond the earth, (heaven) to join the Father and the Holy Spirit. (Nicene Creed.) This does not fit the concept of panentheism. God is not a separate being who created all that exists from outside of, beyond, or separate from that creation. But, the idea that wisdom, or the divine Logos permeates all of existence, is compatible with panentheism. God is Existence, within all, and yet, undefinably, more than all of existence. Wisdom, or cosmic intelligence (Logos) is within existence, as it orders all existence. Albert Einstein, wrote, "My comprehension of God comes from the deeply felt conviction of a superior intelligence that reveals itself in the knowable world." [24]

God as Energy

If God is "Existence" and yet more than existence, one might propose that the source of all existence is energy. Therefore, in some ways, God might be thought of, or experienced, as "Energy." Of course, God is more than energy and more than all of existence. We should not say that God is "part of existence," or that existence is "part of God." God is ALL. God cannot be divided or compartmentalized. Stating that God is energy, or light or love, simply expresses the many ways that we might think of God, or experience God, as "all that exists and more."

If we think about any object, from a tiny grain of sand to the galaxies in the cosmos, we believe that all matter is made up of minute atoms. Similar to our solar system, within each atom is a nucleus, made up of protons and neutrons. Electrons spin around the nucleus billions of times in a millionth of a second. Overstating it simply, this is what creates the mass of every object that exists. Now we ask, what causes the electrons to whirl around the nucleus? It must be some kind of energy. Energy can be thought of as the basis of all matter. Therefore, the source of energy can be thought of as God the Creator, and that energy, therefore, is an expression of God.

We find energy in gravity. It makes things fall to the earth. It keeps the planets and moons in their orbits. Energy is in magnetism. We think of energy in the wind and the tides. Fire is energy, and transmits energy in heat and light. Energy is in our fuel, gas, oil, coal and nuclear fission. Electricity is energy. Energy is what makes our hearts pump blood through our bodies. It makes our cells develop. It sends messages to our brains. It enables us to run and work and think and play. Energy is in every aspect of existence. Traditional prayers often address God as the "creator and sustainer of the world." That means "energy." Prayer transmits the energy of love. (See page 92.) Energy is an expression or manifestation of God. When we experience energy, we experience God.

God as Light

Closely related to the image of God as energy, is the concept of God as "Light." Energy creates light. Throughout the ages, people have compared their ideas about God with light. Darkness, in scripture, is a symbol for death, suffering, ignorance, judgment and sin. Light is a symbol for God, Jesus, faith, wisdom, virtue, resurrection, newness of life and eternal life. In the prologue to his gospel, the author of the fourth gospel ("St. John") wrote that the Word (Logos, referring to Jesus,) "was the true light that enlightens all men." He came into a world of darkness as a light that shines in darkness, a light that darkness could not overpower. ("St. John" 1:1-9.) That "Inner Light," according to Quaker beliefs, is God in every person. Light is a universal symbol for God. In "The Letter to the Hebrews" 1:3, the author wrote, "He (Jesus) is the radiant Light of God's glory and the perfect copy of God's nature." Jesus is divine Light.

Although God is the Inner Light, at times we do not recognize that Light. The prologue to the fourth gospel continues, "He was in the world that had its being through him, and the world did not know him. He came to his own domain and his own people did not accept him." ("St. John" 1:10 -11. Jerusalem Bible.) Jesus was rejected and crucified. The divine Light within us at times becomes clouded, dimmed and hidden. That "blindness" leads us to sin. We are virtuous when we are in the Light. In Jesus, God the Light, was fully present. Jesus is the "Light of the world." ("St. John" 5:12, 8:12.) The Light of God was manifested so completely and absolutely in Jesus, that his followers were overcome with awe and love for him. Any such experience must be expressed in symbols and metaphors. Words are insufficient. It is mystical. It is a mystery.

In an article in "The Saturday Evening Post," written by G.S. Viereck (October 26, 1929,) Albert Einstein was quoted, "I am a Jew, but I am enthralled by the 'luminous' figure of the Nazarene." Einstein recognized the Light of God in Jesus. Others manifest the Light of God, but for a Christian, none as absolutely as Jesus.

In the English language (and others,) when we use the word "enlighten," we may mean to show forth, to explain, to inform, instruct, or to make clear. When we say that we have been "enlightened," it means that we understand. We might respond, "I see." In his hymn, "Amazing Grace," John Newton wrote about his conversion, "I once was lost but now am found, was blind, but now I see." He saw the Light!

When we experience Jesus, we see the Light, bringing to view the meanings of his life and teachings. We become enlightened in the Christian faith. Through meditation, we try to focus on "seeing" God within ourselves, so that in turn, we may see God in all others. This then becomes a motivation for the way that we treat others. It is our basis for morality.

God as Evolution

Traditionally, theologians have defined God as complete, perfect and absolute, to which nothing can be added or taken away. Nothing can be added to or subtracted from absolute perfection. Because God is complete, God must be unchangeable. God has been defined, therefore, as the "Unmoved Mover." If this is true, how can God be involved in the process of all existence, since existence constantly is changing, developing and evolving? I reject the concept of a complete, changeless and static God.

Creation always is evolving. Wisdom is enlightening. Love is deepening. Our personal lives are developing. There is birth, death and new life. Everything that exists is dynamic. That means change. God must be the source of that evolution, since God is Existence itself. All of creation, energy, wisdom, and love take their power, their existence from God. God is the source of all, involved in all, yet greater than all. God, therefore, constantly is evolving as all existence is evolving.

During the last century, the concept of "Process Theology" developed. This departs from traditional beliefs. It states that God is the source of all that exists, and is in the process of becoming all that can be. God changes existence. God also changes and evolves with existence.

The Jesuit paleontologist, Pierre Teilhard deChardin (1881-1955) wrote:

> We may, perhaps, imagine that creation was finished long ago. But that would be quite wrong. It continues in still more magnificent forms in the highest zones of the world. Our role is to complete it, if only by the humble work of our hands.... This is the real meaning and price of our acts. Owing to the interrelation between matter, soul and Christ, we bring part of being, which he desires, back to God in whatever we do. [25]

Father deChardin wrote also, "Lord Christ, you who are divine energy.... It is you who must set me ablaze and transmute me into fire that we may be welded together and made one." [26]

God as Spirit

Through the ages, God has been thought of as Spirit. In the "Old Testament," the concept of God as Spirit is very prominent. Spirit often is compared to wind, *ruach* in Hebrew. The Spirit of God was operative in creation. ("Genesis" one.)

75

The Spirit of God is both within ourselves and all around us, as well as a power beyond us. This concept comes close to the contemporary theory of panentheism. The Spirit inspires us to seek an experience of God. The Spirit leads us to faith. In Christian theology, the Holy Spirit is fully God, as the Holy Trinity is defined as "Father, Son and Holy Spirit." The Spirit is present in all persons and events of life. The Holy Spirit communicates "direct revelation." The Holy Spirit is God working through mankind. In Quaker beliefs, the Holy Spirit and the Inner Light may appear to be similar, but they are not identical concepts.

God as Trinity

Christianity defines God as One, who is experienced in three ways, or three "persons." They are "Father, Son and Holy Spirit." Sometimes the Trinity is expressed as "Creator, Redeemer and Sanctifier." Any attempts to define God are the personal responses that people have had to their experiences of God. Those responses usually are emotional rather than cerebral. We are carried into the realm of mysticism mainly by emotions rather than intellect. God is called by different names and imagined in millions of varieties of expressions in religions and cultures throughout human history. The many ways that people experience God all are subjective and relative. Any study of world religions will affirm that fact. Note that the Hindus say that there is one God, who has thousands of expressions.

The terminology and symbols of traditional, Trinitarian Christianity simply are insufficient. Historically, they were necessary. Many of them, however, are misleading and confusing. I ask the reader to study the Nicene Creed found on pages 174 and 175. Then read excerpts from the Council of Chalcedon, (451 C.E.) on page 171. Do they inspire an experience of God, or bring you any closer to the Christian faith? There is a huge difference between knowing theology and experiencing God. All definitions of God must be considered very insufficient. God is a mystery. It is impossible to define a mystery! But, we can experience God within ourselves and around us. That experience surpasses all scripture and all theological definitions. Creeds and doctrines leave us cold and confused. God can be revealed mystically and directly in the numinous realm. Those revelations are personal and subjective.

The reference to the Trinity in "The Gospel According to St. Matthew" 28:19-20 is considered by many Biblical scholars to have been a much later addition by an editor.

God as Love

Basic to the Christian faith is the belief that God is a power of love. We find this in the Hebrew scriptures such as "Hosea," "Isaiah" and many others. In the "New Testament," God's love dominates every chapter. One might say that Jesus is "Love Incarnate," the human example of divine love. He was a man who loved to the fullest. One of the many Greek words for "love" is *agape*. It means the kind of love that is absolute. It expects nothing in return. It is willing to sacrifice everything for the sake of love for others.

We cannot begin to imagine God. We cannot describe or define God. Those attempts are mystical metaphors. We call God "Spirit," but it is very difficult to imagine or relate to a spirit. Therefore, since the earliest of times, many religions have thought about God as a person, a supreme, all powerful being, who lives somewhere in the sky, and manipulates the events of human life on earth. I repeat, I must reject that notion. It is a creation of a deity in the image of man. It is pure mythology. But how then, can we speak about God as a power of love? As humans, we need to envision a person or even an animal to feel that we are loved. We may believe that our parents, our spouses, our children, our close friends, even our dogs and cats may love us. But how does an impersonal concept of God express love for us?

In order to experience God's personal love for each of us, we need to use the symbol of God as a person, even though we know that God is not a person. But, we need to envision God. Therefore, we call God "Father." That was a common, Jewish image of God during Jesus's time. God becomes for us the symbol of a loving parent. We experience that love in what we know about Jesus through those who experienced him firsthand, his original apostles and followers. Decades later others wrote what they had learned from those who had known Jesus and experienced not only his love, but his faith, his power to forgive, and his reflection of God.

Those who knew Jesus, knew God. The author of "The Gospel According to St. John" portrays Jesus as saying, "If you know me, you know my Father also." ("St. John" 14:7.) "To have seen me is to have seen the Father." ("St. John" 14: 9.) "You must believe me when I say that I am in the Father and the Father is in me." ("St. John" 14:11. Jerusalem Bible.) Jesus is the man, who through his humanity, was the perfect expression of love. Jesus is the human image of God. There-fore, God is love. Aware of the metaphors and symbolisms, we can imagine God as a loving parent, our Father. The Holy Spirit is divine love (energy) working throughout the world, and through the love that we give and receive. God loves each of us personally as God lives within each of us. We know Jesus mystically and experience his love personally. God is the very ground, the foundation and source of our being. This summarizes what we refer to as "The Holy Trinity." We learn this from scripture, but we experience it personally through meditation and direct revelation. Prayer transmits energy of love.

John Yungblut, in his pamphlet, "Speaking as One Friend to Another," wrote:

Unless the mystical consciousness is developed so that there is a profound sense, not only of being one with God, but of being inseparably one with each other, the species is doomed to extinction.... Not only am I my brother's keeper, but I am my brother.... [27] As Friends (Quakers,) we are committed to an 'ethical mysticism.' The love of God that we have experienced demands that we express our answering love for God in the form of loving others. [28]

80

I believe that faith in God as Love requires action. Prayer must become an expression of love. Prayer without action is impotent. Love without action is mere sentimentality. When we say, "I love," it begs the question, "What are you going to do about it?" We cannot physically help everyone for whom we pray, or everyone whom we love. Love, however, demands that we strive to help as many around us and beyond us as is possible. There are many acts of kindness which we can do each day as ways of worshipping God as Love. We can try to forgive those who harm us, and offer them our friendship and help. We can contribute financially to many causes. We can vote, and work politically for what we believe to be right for all people. We can send the energy of our love to empower others through prayer. Love must be expressed in actions. When we act in love, God is working through us. When we love and serve others, we love and serve God.

Bishop John A. T. Robinson wrote:

Jesus is 'the man for others,' the one in whom love has completely taken over, the one who is utterly open to, and united with, the ground of his being. And this life for others, through participation in the being of God, is transcendence. For at this point of love 'to the uttermost' we encounter God, the ultimate 'depth' of our being.... Because Christ was utterly and completely 'the man for others,' because he was love, he was 'one with the Father,' because God is love. [29]

Experiencing God as Love brings one to the realm of faith. Love can be experienced, but not defined. Our emotional responses to love might be articulated in many ways, but words cannot express the personal experiences of love.

As humans, we are caught up in a world which makes forgiveness, acceptance of those who differ from us or even hate us all very difficult, perhaps impossible. *Agape* love is the ideal, the goal to which God within us pushes us to rise. When we fail to acknowledge the Inner Light of God, we fall far short of our ideals, our goals. We are imperfect people. Our very survival seems to demand that we dominate others. This contradicts the ideal of *agape* love.

The Quaker concept of the Inner Light claims that it represents not only the presence of God within all persons, but also the power of God within all humanity. This is called "divine grace." It is only through divine grace that we can try to love as Christ loved, and always loves each of us.

Prayer and Meditation
Entering the Mystical Realm
of the Numinous

In the quietness and peace of meditation we listen, not for our own expressions of self-will, but for God's revelation. Silently and patiently we wait for the Spirit of God to communicate to us what we should know and do. The distinctions between divine revelation and our own self-deceptions will become more apparent as we pray for wisdom. There follows a sense of serenity and joy, even in the midst of many problems and concerns.

A Reasonable Covenant
John G. Macort [30]

When Quakers pray, they speak of it as holding a person or concern "in the Light." This is a beautiful concept of prayer and of God.

Prayer is the transmission to others of the energy (power) created from love.

Prayer and Meditation

A Difficult Change

Many of us are accustomed to imagining God as a divine "person" in heaven, who can determine events among humans on earth. Most of us have been taught this since early childhood, and those images of God have stuck with us throughout our lives. When we pray, many of us still imagine that we are addressing an "old man in the sky," our "Heavenly Father." People still raise their eyes toward the sky when they pray, or speak of "the man upstairs." That image is expressed throughout scripture, in our liturgies, prayers, hymns and sermons. It is ingrained in us. "Our Father who art in heaven."

I constantly find myself praying to a celestial "person," to Father God, as I pray for my family, or for recovery from illness, for protection, a safe journey, or even for finding a lost item or delivering a good lecture. "God help me," we say. "God keep my children safe. God cure me of this ailment. God make this endeavor a success." Or we may thank God for some good experience, a safe trip, or recovery from illness, as if God somehow had guided our automobile or cured our infection or worked with the surgeon to remove a cancer. We may beg God's forgiveness for something that we regret having done or not done. These images have been ingrained in our lives, and there is nothing wrong with them. I try constantly, however, to imagine God as a power within myself when I express these prayers. That can be difficult, because usually we pray with strong emotions about urgent needs. We pray before we think. We do not pray theologically. We pray as we did as children. If this gives us comfort, it may be all right. But it does raise the basic questions about why this "God" answers some prayers but not all. As a non-theist, I have problems with that image of "God."

For many of us, any change in the way that we imagine God can be devastating, leaving us with a huge void. How do we pray? How do we address God, if God is not an anthropomorphic, divine person or supreme being as imagined in theism? How can an impersonal concept of God (panentheism) be thought to love us personally? Whom do we imagine that we are speaking with when we pray, or when we say, "Lord, hear our prayer?" (Certainly, God does not have ears!) These questions may continue to unsettle our faith. The way we pray reflects what we believe. What do we expect from God when we pray?

During the 1960s and 1970s, I taught in the religion departments of a Roman Catholic preparatory school and also at a Roman Catholic university. I was an Episcopal priest, but had that unique privilege as a result of the new emphasis on ecumenism.

At the preparatory school, every class began with a prayer. When I first started teaching, most of the prayers were the "Hail Mary." After some discussions in faculty meetings, we decided that we should add some variety to what had become rote and mechanical. Each teacher was to compose a different prayer to offer each day. After a few weeks, we decided to ask each student to compose a prayer. Some of the prayers that the boys had prepared were beautiful. Others lacked some theological sophistication. A boy might pray that he would pass, or even get an "A" in his math or history test. One football player ended his prayer with the petition that "we beat the hell out of Bishop Fahey," a rival high school. This gave me the opportunity to explain that God is neither a celestial Santa Claus nor a divine puppeteer, who directs the actions of everyone at all times and places. I explained that most prayers of petition really should be asking God to give us faith, wisdom, guidance, patience, and the ability to understand and love others, so that we ourselves will be enabled to do what is right. Prayer may help us to concentrate and to clear our minds to study for a test, but God will not take the test for us, nor will God change our grades to an "A." That is up to each of us. And no. God will not beat the hell out of Bishop Fahey's football team. God does not play football. To my knowledge neither did Bishop Fahey. After all my explanations about prayer, one of the boys replied, "Hey, Father, why don't we just go back to saying the 'Hail Mary?' It's easier." (Faith is not easy!)

Prayer and the "Puppeteer" God

Some of the most difficult questions that my students and my parishioners constantly asked involved our concepts about God. Because we are humans, our understanding of God is very limited. We try to create a concept of God in our own images, and expect God to have human characteristics like our own. God is the ultimate mystery. We must replace the absolutes about God that we have been taught with a sense of mystery and awe. Some of the questions that constantly arise ask why God allows people to suffer. Why is there evil on the earth? What is the use of prayer? To what extent does God get involved in the everyday affairs of each individual all over the world? My only answer is that God is not an "avatar" who at times invades our lives, manipulates our events and determines all things. Then, why pray?

Some of my friends in Ireland, "good 'Irish' Catholics" they would say, believe that God causes everything that happens in their lives. If the supper burns, or the car runs out of petrol, or it rains on a picnic, if we meet a certain person on the street, if a sheep dies, or we find a lost article, God, or some saint must have caused it to happen. When one day in Ireland I brought an elderly lady a bouquet of flowers, she immediately thanked the Blessed Mother for inspiring me to bring them. Then she said that they were a sign from the Blessed Mother that her daughter would visit her that day after a long absence, because her daughter loved that variety of flowers. With all due respect to the old lady, I smiled as if to agree. (Her daughter did not visit her.) Superstition or faith?

The line between faith and superstition is complex. I do not believe in a "puppeteer" God. God does not move each of the billions of people on earth around like toys. If one soldier is killed in battle and his buddy next to him escapes injury, was that God's will? Consider that the mother of the dead soldier had prayed fervently for his safety. The soldier that was uninjured was an atheist. If a person is killed in an automobile accident, was that God's will? I do not think so. Those deaths resulted from the fact that no two objects can occupy the same space at the same time. When that law of physics involves cars or bullets, fatalities may result. God does not make those things happen, nor does God intervene. God does not direct every sperm cell to determine whether John or Mary will be born. That is pure accident. When someone dies, people often say that "God took him." I do not believe that God "takes" people or causes their deaths. We die when, for some physical reasons, our bodies cease functioning. We often hear people say that God saved them from a terrible accident or illness which would have resulted in death. That bothers me. My question is, why then, does God not save everyone? Why does God save some but not others? Think of how those claims might make a person feel who has lost a son or husband in battle. Why him, but not the other person who claimed to have been saved by God from death? Why do some die at age ten while others live to be a hundred? Does God will us to be afflicted by diseases that cause suffering and death at early ages? Do my prayers really keep me from having an automobile accident? The only answer that I can accept is that God does not intervene in our lives. Some might reply that God has reasons for everything that happens to us. They believe that since we cannot understand those reasons, we must accept them, and continue to believe in a loving God. Only God knows what is best for us, despite our own desires and prayers. Personally speaking, I do not accept that answer. It says that we are controlled by the whims of a fickle "God." What, then is the purpose of prayer? Do prayers matter at all?

First, we must accept the fact that we all are mortal. We all are going to suffer and die from some cause at some point in our lives. That is who and what we are. Does God decide when and how our deaths will happen? I do not think so. Accidents, catastrophes and disease strike us randomly, sometimes by our own neglect, at other times arbitrarily with no explanation. I do not believe that God causes those things, nor does God intervene. They are part of our mortal experience in which suffering and death are inevitable. That is the way that animals, who eventually evolved into humans, all exist. Let us stop blaming God for our human condition. Does God care about our pain and anguish and suffering? Yes, I truly believe that God does care. If, as I believe, the man, Jesus Christ is the perfect manifestation of God, then we see through the experiences of Jesus to God. Jesus shared our human nature. He lived and died as one of us. He was a man of love. Jesus revealed God as Love.

To love someone means that we also suffer with that person. Although God does not take us off our crosses, God, in Jesus Christ, joins us on our crosses. This was demonstrated by the suffering and death of Jesus. As we contemplate Jesus suffering on a cross, we can identify with, and imagine some of his pain. I try to do this by meditating upon a crucifix. (I do not mean a cross without the figure of the dying Jesus upon it. For me, ornate or figureless crosses may mock the horror of the crucifixion.) I focus on a crucifix depicting Jesus in agony, with blood streaming from his head and bodily wounds. Vicariously, in meditation, we can identify with Jesus. Jesus suffers with us, as we journey through our mortal lives, which involve both joy and sorrow, pleasure and pain, birth and death. The cross of Jesus obligates us to suffer for, and with each other. That is love in action. That is what prayer is all about.

Does prayer change God's "mind" about us, or influence God to make things happen to us like a divine puppeteer? No. Prayer does not change God. Prayer changes us. Prayer offers us the ability to maintain our faith in a loving God, to endure the suffering common to all mortal beings, and to unite our wills with God's will, as we try to discern it through meditation. Prayer activates the divine power within us to do God's will.

I believe that all of life is made up of energy. God is the source of all positive, good energy. I believe also that there is energy in the human will. My faith tells me that if I will something for myself, there is energy in that act of "willing." That energy can affect my life. Norman Vincent Peale called it "the power of positive thinking." We observe this energy when we speak about a person's "will to live." We often can feel the energy of love or hostility from other people. If I will something for someone else, I believe that positive energy can be transmitted to another person. It can influence me and also people whom I care about, nearby or far away. (Please do not confuse this with voodoo. I am referring only to positive, divine energy.) If my will, or psychic and emotional energy, is based on goodness and love, then I believe that it is combined with divine energy to influence the lives of others, and to influence my own life also. Our love for others, combined with God's absolute love, can be transmitted to others by the energy (power) of prayer. Through prayer, we can empower each other.

In my various parishes, we offered the Sacrament of Healing each week. As I laid my hands upon the heads of those seeking healing, I would envision energy rising from my feet, through my body, into my shoulders, down my arms and through my hands to the person's head. I could feel the energy move from my body to another's. My hands would become warm. Infrared photography indicates that there is a transmission of heat or energy. Prayer is the transmission of wills (energy) in conjunction with divine energy (love) to influence others, individually or as groups as we pray, for example, for the healing of a person or for peace among nations. This is very different from the idea of "telephoning" God and begging God to do something on our behalf, which is how people often conceive of prayer. God does not have us on puppet strings. When our wills are in harmony with God's will of divine love, then we can explain the efficacy of prayer. Prayer enables us to live lives of love, to make the right decisions, and to accept our suffering and mortality with faith and hope.

Serous prayer requires time, concentration and meditation. Think about how a young child might pray. Hearing a child saying prayers can be beautiful. We cannot expect any sophistication, and never should be critical of childish innocence. A five year old girl might pray, picturing God as a kindly old man with a long, white beard, as she remembers God in a painting. She might quickly say, "God bless Mommy and Daddy and my brother George and my sisters Beth and Sarah, and make Sarah be nicer to me and stop teasing me. God bless Grandma and Grandpa Murphy, and make Grandma Jones recover from her stroke. Make Mary invite me to her birthday party. Amen." It is not much different from a letter to Santa Claus.

Now think about the way that we adults often rattle off prayers. It still is as if we are talking to a celestial person or divine being somewhere off in the "heavens," and asking "him" to make certain things happen for us. We "telephone" God with our list of petitions. Look at any liturgical prayer book, and find the "Prayers of the People." We ask God to make things happen as we hope that God will invade our lives and fulfill our wishes. I confess that as a priest I often sped through the liturgy, reading the prayers as fast as I could say them so that I could get through a service within an hour. Liturgical prayers too often are merely words heard or said by rote with very little thought about their meaning. Corporate, liturgical prayer, or prayers offered by clergy during a church service are very different from the concentration and time needed during meditation.

When meditating alone or in a group, it is necessary to set aside a certain amount of time, usually about an hour, in a place where there is silence, with no interruptions or distractions. In order to engage in intercessory prayer, consider the following steps. After addressing and clearing your mind of other concerns, begin to focus on the persons or concerns that are most important to you. Picture each person for whom you are praying. Force yourself to concentrate on that person. Envision the divine energy of love within you. Feel that energy from your toes rise through your entire body. Your nerves may tingle. Your body suddenly may feel filled with the presence and power of God. Then, as you continue your intense focus on that person, send your energy of love to her or him through the divine mystical power that we all possess. This will take time, perhaps five or more minutes. Then move on the next person or concern for whom you want to pray. After an hour of such intercessory prayer you may feel energized, or perhaps exhausted, but truly at peace.

During a lecture a few years ago, I used a symbol to try to explain the differences between theistic prayer to a God beyond ourselves, a divine person or supreme being on one hand, as opposed to prayer as I just have described it, transmitting the divine energy of love directly from within ourselves to others. I used the symbol of a triangle for prayer to a theistic, divine person whom we may visualize as an "old man off in the heavens." We pray to this God, in hope that this God will intervene in human events on earth and make certain things happen. This can be represented by a triangle, prayer moving from us to God and then responses from that God back to others.

The symbol that I used for direct prayer is a straight line. We visualize God as a presence and power within ourselves. Then we focus upon another person or concern. Mystically, with strong concentration and energy, we transmit the divine love within us to another person, or to our concerns. I believe, from research into early Quakers, that their concept of prayer was much more like this description. God is within us.

I realized, however, that my symbolism was faulty when one of my students said, "Oh, we just leave out the middle man." No, that is not what I meant. This does not leave God out of the process, but rather it recognizes God within ourselves and all others. God is not a "middle man." God is within us, within all that exists, and yet greater than all that exists. But, according to this belief, there is a direct line (transmission) of divine energy from one person to another. We are not asking God "up there" to intervene for us by directing events on the earth. God is both immanent (within us,) and transcendent (beyond us.) That is panentheism.

We think of the "Inner Light" as the presence of God within all persons. But, we also need to recognize that "God-within-us" means that we possess divine power as well as divine presence. We may feel little power over our weaknesses, our temptations, our propensities to do what is harmful, over our physical drives and our struggles for survival in competition with others. They all can overwhelm us. It is easy to fall into a trap of feeling helpless victims of the forces of evil. But, we do have divine power within us to do what is right and fair, what we believe to be fulfilling the will of God as love (*Agape*.) We are God's instruments on earth. God enables us to create relationships of love and respect for all people, for nature and the universe. We are called to be God's peacemakers. These are our missions, our obligations as Christians. We pray for the power of God to work through us. Prayer transmits that divine power in us to others.

Prayer as meditation or contemplation can mean "listening" to the Holy Spirit, that of God within us, as we try to discern what truly is the will of God for us. That "waiting on the Spirit" as the Quakers call it, takes discipline and time. That is one reason why I find it helpful to attend Friends Meetings. It is more important to try to discover God's will for each of us, than it is to keep begging

God for what we think we want or need. Prayer should be thought of as listening to God more than speaking to God. We experience God. We do not create a "God" to fulfill our personal desires. By seeking God within ourselves, we come to know who we are and who God is. We learn about each other also, and what we need to do to express love to others around us and throughout the world. This comes from deep, disciplined meditation, when, finally we "Center Down" on an awareness from our innermost beings. We mystically enter the numinous realm, and feel the direct revelation and presence of God within ourselves, the Inner Light.

We say that God reveals divine will to us through the Holy Spirit. That "divine will" has been articulated by various people through the writings of scripture, or through the Christian Church, or by individuals. It comes to us also through personal, direct revelation in the mystical realm of the numinous. It becomes obvious, however, that individuals and denominations dis-agree over their beliefs concerning the will of God.

During the American Civil War, there were those in the Confederacy who pointed to the Bible to justify slavery. They prayed fervently for a Confederacy victory. In India, many British prayed in Anglican churches that the British

Empire would remain as the rulers of India, while Mohandas Gandhi, (a Hindu and truly a "Godly" man,) peacefully led the nation to independence. Today there are Christian denominations that point to scripture to justify discrimination against homosexuals, or call their sexual relations sinful. Other denominations have clergy who are openly in homosexual relationships, and bless those unions as marriages. I have served parishes that supported Planned Parenthood with substantial contributions from their outreach funds. Yet other Christians make anti-abortion one of their top priorities. They pray that all abortions will be outlawed. They all read the same <u>Bible</u> and worship the same God. We cannot presume that God always is on our side. My point is, that when an individual, or a denomination or religion claims to know God's will absolutely and universally, I find any such declarations to be presumptuous, naïve, impossible and invalid. (I hope that the days of the Inquisition are over!)

Perhaps God reveals divine will to us personally and corporately. I believe so. But, as Saint Paul wrote, we all see it as through a dark, distorted mirror. Does that apply to the writers of scripture, or to Church doctrines concerning issues of faith and morals? I believe that it does. It applies also to our personal, subjective interpretations of our direct revelation experiences. No one can set himself or herself up as God, neither can any religion, book or human authority. Through prayer, however, we search, in our limited ways, trying to discover what might be right for us individually, or corporately, as a family, a Church or a nation. We may look to scripture, doctrine and Church teachings for inspiration and guidance, but these are human opinions. No persons can claim to have the absolute truth, or attempt to impose their authority upon others who disagree. This is where compromise, respect, love, and the recognition of God in every person must be foremost in all relationships, in all religious traditions, nations, politics and beliefs.

When individuals, religions, denominations or nations claim that their interpretations of God's will is the only correct way for everyone, universally, I call that blasphemy. It puts human opinions above God. Prayer opens us to experiencing God each in our own personal ways. We do not control God through prayer. Neither does God control us. Nor should we, or anyone, attempt to control each other in the name of God. That is one of the problems with proselytizing. It says that we are right and you are wrong. That is one reason why Quakers do not proselytize. Missionaries should try to serve rather than convert. Conversions can result from their examples of love.

Am I saying that everything is relative in terms of human faith and moral values? It doesn't take an anthropologist to answer that question. As cultures, religions, denominations and individuals differ widely on issues of faith and morals, who and what is correct? Some may decide this either individually, or by associating with a religious or political organization with which they personally agree, and to which they offer their allegiance. That allegiance then becomes a matter of personal choice. Others are conditioned from childhood to believe certain things, and they remain faithful to that conditioning. Do not expect a Muslim in Iraq, therefore, to pray for the same things as a Christian in the United States. I believe that there is only one God. But, God goes by different names in many religions and cultures.

Why pray at all if God does not get involved in the events of human lives? God is involved in all aspects of human life because God is within every human person. God is love. God is the Inner Light within us. When Quakers speak about praying for someone or some concern, they say that they are holding that person or concern "in the Light." Prayer transmits the energy of God's love, the Inner Light, from us to others. Prayer in action is love. It is caring about others, and sharing their gratitude, their hopes, their suffering and sorrow on the deepest level of relationships. Prayer unites us to each other. Quaker prayer is listening, opening one's awareness to the divine Light within. It is contemplation, a patient waiting for revelations which enlighten us in ways to act, to serve, to sacrifice, to do God's will, to bring peace and love to everyone throughout the world. Prayer should initiate actions of love for all people!

Excerpts from prayers in the
1979 Book of Common Prayer
of the Episcopal Church
of the United States of America.

O God of peace, who has taught us that...quietness and confidence shall be our strength: By the might of thy Spirit lift us, we pray thee, to thy presence, where we may be still and know that thou art God.   (Page 832.)

Deliver us, when we draw near to thee, from coldness of heart and wandering of mind, that with steadfast thoughts and kindled affections we may worship thee in spirit and in truth.   (Page 833.)

O God, who dost manifest to thy servants the signs of thy presence: Send forth upon us the Spirit of love, that in companionship with one another thine abounding grace may increase among us, through Jesus Christ our Lord.   (Page 71.)

102

SCRIPTURE

The best, and perhaps only ways that we can describe our faith are through myths, legends, symbols, rituals, liturgies, art, drama, poetry, music, or dance. Mere words do not suffice.

Reading scripture literally turns most of the Christian religion into irrational mythology.

"There is no use trying," said Alice. "One cannot believe impossible things."

Lewis Carroll, <u>Alice in Wonderland</u>.

Why do most Quakers emphasize "direct revelation" over scripture and doctrine?

(Refer also to pages 25 - 34.)

Scripture

The Bible is not the word of God. In fact, it is made up mostly of myths and legends. It is not history or science. It cannot be used to predict the future or to influence morality for our contemporary society. Its words were not dictated literally by God to its authors. Scripture never was written to be understood as literal, historic truth. Enjoy its beautiful parables and allegories.

Whatever was taught and believed two or three thousand years ago, may not be valid if applied to situations today. Scripture should be taken seriously, but not literally or out of context. One never should point to "proof texts" in scripture to justify a decision today, especially regarding prophecies about the future or laws or certain moral issues. We live in a very different age from those who wrote the chapters of scripture. Issues such as slavery, equality for women, dietary and dress rules, sexuality, marriage, divorce and scores of other subjects cannot be judged by the ways that people thought about them centuries ago. The Bible has been misused to justify almost anything, good or evil. It may offer guidelines and inspiration, but must be read critically and within the historical context of each author. The legends and parables, however, are necessary for our understanding of the deeper, mystical meanings of scripture.

Scripture can be called "the word of God" only because it is about God. The "God" that it describes may not present the same theological picture that many can accept today. God did not create the world in six days. There is no place called heaven above the earth or hell beneath it. There were no Adam and Eve, no Garden of Eden. The first humans did not "fall" out of favor with God. Moses did not write the Pentateuch. There was no Tower of Babel. There were no divinely inflicted plagues in Egypt, nor was there a miraculous parting of the Red Sea to allow the Hebrew people to escape the pharaoh's armies. There was no Noah's ark. Methuselah did not live for 969 years, and Jonah did not live in the stomach of a whale. Sodom and Gomorrah were not destroyed because of immorality. Lot's wife was not turned into a pillar of salt. Elijah did not ride to heaven in a chariot.

All these stories were part of the Hebrew epic. They were similar to the epics such as Homer's "Iliad" and "Odyssey" or Virgil's "Aeneid," telling the legends of ancient Greece and Troy. In England, there is the epic of King Arthur. There probably was a King Arthur, but historically no one really knows all of his adventures, certainly not all of those written by Thomas Malory in his *Le Morte Darthur*. The legendary outlaw Robin Hood of the 14th century who robbed the rich and gave to the poor may have been a historic person, but hundreds of legends have grown up about him from the 14th century through our contemporary television programs. Much the same can be said about figures such as Davy Crocket and Daniel Boone in United States history. They were real men in history, but the legends that developed about them fill many books and television episodes. Similar things can be said about many of the characters in the "Old Testament." It is a collection of some history, but mostly told as stories filled with mythology, legends, parables, metaphors and hyperbole. It is the Hebrew epic.

Much the same can be said of the Christian gospels. From the earliest non-Christian sources, we know from the Jewish historian Josephus , who wrote in *circa* 90 C.E., "…that a man named Jesus of Nazareth lived and was crucified by Pontius Pilate. Jesus had a group of followers which has continued to grow significantly."[31] (Paraphrased.) That much we know for sure about the historic Jesus. We cannot be absolutely certain about very much more.

None of the authors of the four gospels knew Jesus personally, neither did Saint Paul. They all were writing from what they had heard from others, decades later. All the books of the "New Testament" were written in Greek. None of Jesus's original apostles would have been fluent enough in Greek to have written them. They spoke Aramaic. Early texts once existed which are believed to have recorded many of Jesus's sayings. They were written before any of the four gospels, but now are lost. The most famous is called the "Quelle Document." (Also called "Q.") It was a collection of oral traditions that were gathered from various sources and written down. The authors of the gospels of "St. Matthew" and "St. Luke" must have had access to "Quelle" and inserted much of it into their writings. In verses where Matthew and Luke are nearly identical, one may assume that each independently copied them from the "Quelle Document." I suggest that those verses may be fairly original and accurate. Matthew and Luke copied much of their texts also from the earliest canonical gospel, "St. Mark."

Although the authors of the "New Testament" never had known Jesus, they were greatly inspired by those who had known him decades before, and they were excited by stories that they had heard about him. Jesus's original followers had been overwhelmed by the experience of his presence with them. Then they continued to experience his presence after his crucifixion. They were willing to give every part of their lives, even to execution, for his sake. Later, that enthusiasm was passed on to the authors of the "New Testament" and to those who then called themselves followers of Jesus. The overwhelming awe and enthusiasm of those who originally and personally had known him could not be explained in words. Therefore, all sorts of legends and stories grew up to try to convey to later generations what an enormous impact Jesus had on those who originally had followed him. This is the key to understanding scripture, whether it refers to the great patriarchs and prophets of the Hebrews, or to the person of Jesus, or later, to various saints. The stories in scripture are responses to the original experiences of people before them. Therefore, for decades, or centuries after those original experiences, people passed on legends and myths, usually with great exaggerations. Each generation added its own versions. There were legends upon legends upon legends. Finally, many of these were written down in what now is called the Hebrew and Christian scriptures.

We may think on a much lesser scale of George Washington and Abraham Lincoln. Some people of their day who had known those men personally must have had tremendous respect for them, for their honesty and integrity. How could they express their enthusiasm? They did so by telling legends that young George Washington confessed to his father that he had cut down a cherry tree, because he could not tell a lie. A story grew up about how young Abraham Lincoln, while working as a clerk in a shop, ran for miles after a customer to give him a few pennies that Lincoln believed he had short changed the man. Did these incidents happen? Who knows? Probably not. But, they have left generations of Americans with a belief in the honesty and integrity of those men. The impressions that Jesus made on his followers while he lived with them was much more overwhelming than that of any other person that I can imagine. They can be expressed only in myths, legends and hyperbole.

When reading scripture, one always must be aware of the fact that each author had his own agenda. What was it that the author wanted to stress? The authors of the chapters in both the Hebrew and Christian scriptures each were trying to convince their readers to accept certain beliefs or points of view. Those agendas might have been to convince the readers that a particular prophet was especially great, or that they must obey certain laws of the Torah, or that God might punish them, or that God would lead them out of exile. The Hebrew scriptures are filled with different points of view of the various authors, sometimes in conflict with each other. Also, remember that scripture does not always present history in chronological order. The first chapter of "The Book of Genesis" for example, was written at least a century after the second chapter of "Genesis." "The Book of Deuteronomy" was written decades after the rest of the Pentateuch.

Reading the different chapters about the same events in history might be similar to reading two versions about the American Civil War, one written by a Union sympathizer, and the other by a Confederate. Each author would have his own agenda. Each account will be different. Within the "Old Testament," one finds many different versions of stories, some from the northern land of Israel, others from the southern land of Judah. Later still, other similar stories were written by authors centuries after the earliest. Each author had something different to prove to his readers.

In the "New Testament," the main goal of the authors of the epistles and gospels was to prove that Jesus of Nazareth indeed was the Jewish messiah. He was the fulfillment of the law and the prophets. He was God Incarnate, that is, the perfect manifestation of God. Each author had a distinct agenda. Each was writing to a different audience, from a subjective point of view and a particular set of circumstances.

The Hebrew people of Jesus's time were known for hyperbole or exaggerations in narrating or writing about their history. How does one express awe, mystery, overwhelming, unique experiences? Even every superlative adjective becomes inadequate. Therefore, we exaggerate. When my sons were about five and six years old, I took them to see the circus. When they came home, I overheard them telling their friends that people were flying through the air without ropes, 50 dwarfs got out of a tiny car, elephants were jumping through hoops, and a woman had a poisonous snake wrapped around her neck. Of course, these all were exaggerations, but that was the only way that the boys could express their enthusiasm about what they had seen in the circus. After telling many of their friends about it, they came to believe it all themselves. Think about these things when reading how the authors of the scriptures described the events of Hebrew history, and the great "giants" of faith whom they revered so highly from their past, kings, leaders, prophets, and later, for Christians, Jesus Christ.

Who Was the Real Jesus?

"Where there is smoke, there is fire!" Where there are legends and exaggerations in scripture, there must have been magnificent, unique, awe-inspiring persons who caused such responses. There had to have been very powerful original sources of all the legends that were passed on.

Most "New Testament" scholars agree that Jesus did not actually say verbatim most of the words that are attributed to him in the gospel accounts. The author of each gospel took whatever information he might have heard from oral traditions or older writings, and created a narrative to reflect what the author imagined that Jesus might have said or done. Each author of a gospel had his own particular and unique image of Jesus.

It is difficult to determine which of the miracles that Jesus was alleged to have performed are actual, historic accounts. Which are legends or extreme exaggerations? Certainly, Jesus actually did perform many "miracles." He was known as a healer, of which there were many during his time. Jesus tried not to call attention to himself when he performed miracles. This may have been for three reasons.

First, Jesus did not want to anger the conservative Jewish or the Roman authorities who would have been threatened by his popularity as a miracle worker. That would have been dangerous. Second, as was expressed in his "temptations," Jesus did not want his followers to have faith in him simply because he could work miracles. ("St. Matthew" 4:1-10.) Third, during Jesus's time, there were numerous miracle workers and sorcerers. "Acts" 8:9-24 tells of one named Simon Magus, who was rebuked by St. Peter. Jesus did not want the reputation of being a sorcerer. He wanted people to follow him for reasons more profound than being charmed by miracles.

Before Jesus's followers experienced his presence after his death, Jesus eventually may have been thought of as the messiah, but never did he or any of his followers think of him as divine. That would be the most serious heresy that a Jew could commit. Jesus and his contemporary followers lived and died as Jews. Any thoughts of Jesus being divine did not arise until many of his followers had experienced him alive after his crucifixion. Any references to Jesus's divinity while he lived are the words of later writers, and not those of Jesus or of his contemporary followers. The same is true for references to the Trinity, such as in "St. Matthew" 28:19-20.

We are left with questions about how we imagine Jesus. In order to focus our meditation on him, we may need some image or picture in our minds. Everyone will experience Jesus in different and very personal ways. That is important to remember. But, some Christians claim that their responses to Jesus, and to God, are the only true and acceptable beliefs for all who call themselves Christians. Serious problems result.

Some may picture God as an old man in the heavens, looking down and moving each person around like a toy soldier. I do not. Some may think of God as angry and vengeful because of our sins. I do not. Some may picture Jesus's birth in a stable in Bethlehem. I do not. Some may imagine Jesus as he has been portrayed in some old films, effetely, blond, Anglo-Saxon, speaking sanctimoniously in Shakespearean English. I do not. Some may picture the child Jesus dressed in silk, and wearing a crown over his curly blond hair. I do not. Some may think of Jesus as more divine than human, as God masquerading on earth as a human being. I do not. We all have different images of God and of Jesus that are very subjective and personal. Since no one really knows what the historical Jesus looked like, or what he actually said and did, we all may imagine Jesus in different ways. We know that Jesus was a first century Jew. Even that has been obscured by some. I believe that his image as divine has overshadowed his humanity. My question is, therefore, has the real Jesus, the man Jesus of Nazareth, been lost in all of the later legends, the myths, creeds and popular images? I believe so.

Consider, as a rather insufficient analogy, the story of Saint Nicholas of Bari, Bishop of Myra. He lived in the fourth century C.E. Some might recognize St. Nicolas only because of his association with legends about Father Christmas, Santa Claus or St. Nick. For most people, the story of St. Nicholas of Bari, Bishop of Myra, has been lost.

St. Nicholas was famous and revered for being an extremely generous bishop of an impoverished diocese. His parents had died when he was a young man, leaving him a good sum of money. He was determined to devote his inheritance to helping the poor. In the nearby town of Patara, there lived a man who had lost all his money. He had three daughters to support. Because his daughters were so impoverished, they could not find husbands. Such poverty often meant that young women were forced into menial labor or prostitution to support themselves. Nicholas realized that the father of these girls was a very hard working, honorable man, who had lost his money through no fault of his own. Secretly, Nicholas threw a bag of gold into an open window of the man's house. This provided a dowry for the eldest daughter. She soon was married. Then, in time, Nicholas did the same for the second and the third daughters. Eventually all were married to fine gentlemen. St. Nicholas's Day is celebrated in December. It was from this story that, centuries later, legends grew up about Father Christmas or Santa Claus, who brings gifts to children. (From this story also developed the placing of three golden balls over the doors of pawn shops.) All of this started with a response to the great generosity of St. Nicholas. For those who know the story, the memory of St. Nicholas is kept alive. The problem is, that in many cases the original source that inspired these legends is forgotten. When most people think of "Saint Nick" they think of Santa Claus, bringing gifts. The real St. Nicholas, known for his generous gifts, has all but been forgotten. Consider how the real meanings of Christmas have been obscured by all of the emphasis upon the legends that developed about Jesus's conception and birth in a stable in Bethlehem. The meaning of Christmas is that a child, born of a man and a woman, grew to become the human image of God, the God of Love for all humanity. Our greatest gift is knowing the real Jesus, mystically, each in our own ways.

Fundamentalism

Christian fundamentalism began in the late 19th century among some British and American Protestants. It was a reaction against "modernist" theologians who rejected certain doctrines, especially the inerrancy of the <u>Bible</u>. Fundamentalists, often called "evangelicals," dominate many conservative denominations. Fundamentalism became active around 1910-1920, when some conservative Protestant theologians published a twelve-volume set of essays to define and defend what they considered to be Protestant orthodoxy. They condemned critical research of scripture, and declared that the <u>Bible</u> was true absolutely as the word of God. In addition to Biblical inerrancy, they also demanded absolute, literal belief in the virginal conception of Jesus by the virgin Mary and the Holy Spirit. They believed the substitutionary theory of the Atonement. (Jesus died as a substitute to pay God for the sins of humanity. See page 139-140, Anselm.) They insisted on the physical resurrection of Jesus's body and on the second coming of Christ. I strongly disagree with every one of these doctrines as they are defined traditionally and literally by many, perhaps most, Trinitarian Christians. Each of these doctrines will be discussed and repudiated in later chapters.

Conservative Roman Catholics have their own forms of similar demands for orthodoxy. In August 1950, Pope Pius XII issued the encyclical *Humani Generis*, condemning several modern, intellectual movements and tendencies in the Christian Church. It condemned existentialism (situation ethics,) much of critical Biblical analysis, and "undue freedom in interpretation." Although it allowed for the possibility of evolution, it stated that original sin reaches us directly from Adam and Eve. Those papal encyclicals and Protestant fundamentalism have kept Christianity in ignorance about the truth of how scripture was written, and they have defied all scientific research, secular and religious. They have made Christianity unbelievable for thousands of people. They have turned the Christian faith into a religion that no rational, intelligent person should respect or take seriously, except to realize the tragic harm that it has done to so many naive believers.

The fundamentalists believe that they have the only absolute truth about Christianity, and everyone who differs from them is wrong and damned. They turn a religion of love and acceptance into a horrible system of legalism, judgment, exclusion, hatred and damnation. All of this is done "in the name of God." To me, that is a terrible abomination!

Consider the harm, the, abuse, the hatred, discrimination, the emotional fear and turmoil that people have suffered from absolute, literal interpretations of scripture and doctrines. They demand adherence to laws, many of which are trivial, harmful and outdated, from cultures and times thousands of years ago. Think of the harm done to minorities, to people of different faiths, to women, children, homosexuals, Muslims, Jews and others throughout history, all based on irrational interpretations of scripture. These abuses continue to play a strong role in American politics, supported by right-wing evangelicals and "social-issue" conservatives. Efforts for peace, for justice, aid to the impoverished, to immigrants, universal health care, equal rights for all minorities, women's reproductive rights all are put aside in favor of "conservative" religious and political agendas. They believe that everyone who differs from them in religion or politics poses a threat to their values, faith and freedom. Think of what Islamic fundamentalists have done to distort the Muslim faith. When I think of fundamentalists of any religion, I remember the words of Alfred, Lord Tennyson in "Maud", Pt. 1, XXII:

But the churchmen fain would kill their church, as churches have killed their Christ.

"The Word of God?" NO!

In his book, <u>Sins of Scripture</u>,[32] Bishop John Shelby Spong summarized some of the horrible statements in scripture which many fundamentalists call "the Word of God." I shall list a few from various sources.

"Deuteronomy" 21:18-21 says that if a son is rebellious against his parents, he shall be stoned to death. "Deuteronomy" 22:20-21 says that if a man marries a woman who cannot show evidence of her virginity, her father shall be flogged and fined. If her lack of virginity is substantiated, she shall be stoned to death. Chapter 22:22 states, "If a man is caught sleeping with another man's wife, both must die." "Exodus" 21:7 says that it is permissible for a man to sell his daughter into slavery. "Exodus" 20:17 assumes that a man's wife is his possession, like his ox and donkey. "Joshua" 10:12-15 claims that God stopped the sun in the sky so that Joshua would have time to kill more of his enemies.

In "First Samuel" 15:3, Samuel orders King Saul, "in the name of God," to kill men, women and infants. "Psalms" 137:8-9 says, "Blessings on him who dashes your babies against a rock." "Proverbs" 23:13-14 advises, "Do not withhold discipline from a child…. If you beat him with a rod you will save him from sheol." "First Corinthians" 11:2-16 refers to the myth of Adam and Eve to prove that women are inferior to men, and therefore must be subject to their husbands. "Leviticus" 20:13 states, "If a man lies with a male as with a woman, both of them have committed an abomination; they shall be put to death." In "The Gospel According to St. Matthew," the author depicts a Jewish crowd responding to Pilate's plea that Jesus was innocent, with the words, "His blood be on us and on our children," meaning the Jews. ("Matt." 27:25.) "Colossians" 3:22 says that slaves must obey their masters. Finally, the author of "The Gospel According to St. John" claimed that Jesus had said, "No one comes to the Father but by me." ("St. John" 14:6.) I do not believe that Jesus ever said those words.

If one interprets scripture and doctrine literally, historically, factually, as we understand those definitions, then the entire treasure of the Christian faith is lost in a sea of contradictions, unbelievable accounts, mythological tales, all of which defy science and reason. They lead to skepticism and disbelief. It all becomes fiction. For me, calling those statements "the word of God" is unacceptable. Bibliolatry is idolatry. It claims that the words of men are the words of God.

The Three-Storied Universe

From ancient times, until the times of Copernicus (1473-1543) and later Galileo, it was assumed that the world was flat and was the center of the universe. The sun, moon, planets and stars revolved around the earth. The earth was like a saucer floating on a tub of water which surrounded it and flowed beneath it. Somewhere there existed "sheol," the place where the dead slept or existed in a kind of unconscious state, awaiting a general resurrection. Later, the idea of hell was taken from other religions. Hell existed as a place of horrible punishment somewhere under the earth. Dante Alighieri, around 1330 C.E., published his <u>Divine Comedy</u>. His "Inferno," his "Purgatorio," and "Paradiso" popularized the notions of hell, purgatory and heaven.

People believed that above the earth, somewhere in the sky, was heaven. That was a place where those who were deemed worthy of such a reward lived with God after death. It was the domain of God, a heavenly, divine being, who created and sustains the universe, who intervenes in the events of humanity on earth, and judges all persons after their deaths. The belief in a judgment and punishments or rewards for the ways that individuals lived on earth, offered a comfortable answer to the question of why some people get away with evil, while other righteous people suffer. People invented humanistic answers to solve unexplainable mysteries about injustice and mortality. They believed that this celestial "God" manipulated all the events of human life, good and bad. This portrays a very anthropomorphic image of the divine. All those images must be rejected, for me at least, in order to hold to a reasonable and believable faith.

When we hear words such as, "Our Father, who art in heaven," or statements from the Nicene Creed (page 174) which say that Jesus "came down from heaven," or "he is seated at the right hand of the Father," or "he descended into hell," or he "ascended into heaven," we must remember that these were written by Christians centuries ago who believed in a three-storied universe. (Consider also the Roman Catholic dogma of the assumption of Mary into heaven.) I realize that those words are symbolic. They must be understood as metaphors. For me, they sound like ancient Greek mythology. Mystically, I dwell upon God within myself, in others and in everything that exists. Should we change? How? Those words are welded to traditional Christian faith. They are not a problem for most Christians. They are for me! I have difficulty affirming them.

Corporate Identity

One very important concept to understand about the Hebrew-Christian mentality is corporate identity and corporate guilt. Very common among many ancient cultures was the belief that everyone in a community was held responsible for whatever any other member of the group did. Responsibility could be transferred from one person to another. One man might have committed a crime, but because he was an important member of the tribe, perhaps a strong warrior or a chief, some other man might be punished in his place, even though that man was innocent. The Hebrews believed that if a king disobeyed God, the entire nation would be guilty and would deserve punishment. Conversely, a high priest, or perhaps a king, could take upon himself responsibility for the actions of any members of the tribe. One person could die to pay a penalty for all. In much of Hebrew history, divine retribution was placed upon the entire nation rather than directed at individuals.

In the minds of many primitive tribes, guilt could be transferred to an animal as well as to other persons. The animal actually could become a substitute for a person or for an entire community. This was the basis for animal sacrifice in the temple in Jerusalem. People offered animals as sacrifices for their own sins. On the Day of Atonement, the high priest would take upon himself the sins of all the Hebrew people. Having sacrificed a bull or a goat on the altar, the priest would take a second goat, called the *azazel* or scapegoat. The priest would place his hands upon the head of the scapegoat, and transfer to the goat all the sins of the Hebrew people. The scapegoat then embodied all the corporate sins of the Hebrew people. The goat was driven into the desert to die, thereby expelling all the guilt for the sins of the people. In much the same way, a Pascal lamb was offered to God on Passover, representing all the Hebrew people. Later, Jesus was called the "Lamb of God," a sacrifice for all human sin. This all is primitive mythology. I reject it.

Fallout from the Fall

As I see it, perhaps the most historically destructive chapters of scripture are "Genesis" two through four. These tell the myth of Adam and Eve, and their "fall" from God's favor. That myth is the basis of later doctrines of original sin and the depravity of all of humanity. It tells of the separation of mankind from God. It has led to all kinds of ridiculous and unfortunate doctrines, from original sin to Calvinistic predestination to

Roman Catholic Marian dogmas. These are based on the concept of corporate guilt, which was claimed to have been passed on from Adam and Eve to all of humanity. From it also developed the theory of the substitutionary Atonement, meaning that Jesus took upon himself the sins of all of humanity when he died to redeem the faithful by appeasing an angry God. Horrible mythology!

Probably everyone knows the myth of Adam and Eve in the Garden of Eden. Supposedly, they were the first people whom God created. Adam was created first, and then Eve was created from one of Adam's ribs. They were perfect people, innocent of any ideas about good or evil, except for one stipulation. They could not eat any fruit from "the tree of knowledge of good and evil." If they did eat from that tree, they would become mortal and eventually die. God had created animals. A serpent tempted Eve to eat the forbidden fruit, which she did. Then Eve tempted Adam to eat some also. Immediately, they realized that they were naked. Obviously, there are sexual symbols in the story. (Tragically, throughout Christian history, sexual relations have been associated very much with sin.) When God realized that Adam and Eve had eaten the forbidden fruit, God decreed curses upon them. The snake will be accursed more than all other beasts. It will have to crawl on its belly. Eve, and all women after her, will be inflicted with great pain during childbirth. Women will be submissive to men. Men will have to labor hard for food. Everyone eventually will die. Our corpses will return to dust. Adam and Eve were banished from the Garden of Eden. They would have to decide what was right or wrong, good or evil. ("Genesis" three.) They had sexual relations, and two sons were born. One son, Cain, a farmer, killed his brother Abel, a shepherd. Now sin had entered the world. There would be enmity between farmers and shepherds. Women would be known as those who tempt men. (The myth observes that whenever an authority forbids people from doing something, they become more tempted to break that prohibition. Also noted by Saint Paul.)

In their attempts to answer some basic questions about life, people in every culture have invented myths. Why do we suffer pain and sickness? Why do we grow old? Why do women suffer such pain during childbirth? Why are we plagued with poisonous snakes, insects and dangerous animals? Why do people die? If God is so perfect, why is God's creation so imperfect? Is God responsible for creating evil, death, sickness, suffering, wars, injustice and all the negative aspects of our mortal lives? There are so many questions. The myths in "Genesis" two and three tried to address some of those questions. Their responses have caused some serious theological problems. Again, theologians have tried to build upon the Adam and Eve myths, using methods of logic, which mean that each theory must lead to a rational conclusion. Myths do not work that way.

Some have suggested that there is a dualism of powers, one that is good and another that is evil. The good and the evil forces always are in conflict with each other, and they inflict their influence upon humanity. This theory can be found in the Hebrew-Christian traditions also as God versus Satin (Lucifer, the Devil.) These are mythological inventions to explain the human struggle between good and evil. (See "Zoroastrianism.")

The "Genesis" story portrays a perfect, eternal creation by a perfect, benevolent God. Because of human disobedience to God's one stipulation, all of creation lost its eternal perfection. Sickness, hard labor for survival, pain, suffering, injustice, murder, death, and moldering corpses all resulted. Humans became estranged from God. The entire creation "fell" from perfection to the difficult state of "sin," suffering and evil that we experience in our lives. That is a horrible myth. There was no such "fall."

128

One problem with the doctrine of our "fallen nature" is its false assumption that a perfect God must have created a perfect world. God could not be responsible for human imperfection, evil and mortality. But, God did not create a perfect world. Humanity and creation, by nature, always have been imperfect. We are not perfect gods. By definition, our lives are finite. That is who and what we are. We suffer pain. We grow old. We die. Our corpses decay. We live in a condition of survival of the fittest within creation and among animals and humans. There is a food chain in which the weak are overcome by the stronger species. That is necessary for survival. That is the way creation works. Finitude and mortality are parts of our human condition. Everything is evolving from life to death to new life. We want to be eternal, like God. But, we are imperfect humans, not gods. The "original sin," as I interpret it, was that humans wanted to be equal to God, perfect and immortal. (Consider also the myth of Lucifer, who would not serve God in John Milton's <u>Paradise Lost</u>. See "Revelation" twelve.)

God does not inflict suffering or evil upon us, nor does a mythological evil force such as Satin influence us to do evil deeds. Our propensity to be selfish and to defend ourselves from others is part of our desire for survival. When we fail to recognize the Light of God within ourselves and within others, we become threatened, angry, vengeful, hateful, and take our frustrations out on others. This leads to crimes, poverty, murder, wars and social chaos. We have free will. We can do good or evil. We are responsible, to a certain extent, for what we do, for what happens to us, and for how we respond to our human condition. These all are determined by the conditions around us, the choices that we make, or the choices that others make. We may have little power over many of the evil conditions that are inflicted upon us. We do, however, have choices in how we respond. We can rise above our animal instincts. But, we need God's power within us, the Inner Light.

Finally, if God is within us, we never really can be separated from God. We do, however, often ignore the presence of God within us and within each other. That is not God's fault. It is a problem that comes from being imperfect and flawed. That has been the evolutionary process of natural selection in human development. Our responses to challenges in life can be good or evil. Evil can dominate our lives, or we can use the divine power within us to make the right choices and respond in virtuous, loving ways. I believe, with most Quakers, that humans are basically good because the Light of God is within us.

Original Sin

Looking back at the concepts of corporate identity or guilt, and literalizing the myth of Adam and Eve, early Christian theologians developed the theory of "original sin." This theory is the basis for a huge amount of Christian doctrines, which I reject, believing them to be false and very unfortunate. The concept had its roots in St. Paul's epistles, but it was literalized and popularized by Saint Augustine, and later by Roman Catholics and especially Protestant, John Calvin.

St. Augustine became the Bishop of Hippo in the year 396. In those days, only bishops could administer the Sacrament of Baptism. Because of primitive travel conditions, many years would elapse between a bishop's visits to distant areas of his diocese. Many unbaptized people, especially infants, would die before a bishop could return to baptize. The question arose as to whether infants should be baptized while the bishop was present baptizing older children and adults. Baptism was the necessary initiation for anyone to become a Christian. Part of the meaning of Baptism was to cleanse a person from past, personal sins. Little children, however, could not be considered responsible for committing deliberate sins. How then could one justify baptizing an infant?

At that time, Augustine was embroiled in a controversy with a British monk named Pelagius. Pelagius was teaching that mankind could rise above the power of sin to do what is right without the help of God's grace. Augustine believed that because of mankind's fallen nature, only through the power of the Holy Spirit can anyone do what is right. Augustine, and other like-minded theologians, proposed that after Adam and Eve disobeyed God in the Garden of Eden, all of humanity inherited their sin. For many reasons, I disagree with Augustine. First, he literalized a myth as if it were historically true. Second, I do not believe that mankind "fell" from God's grace and needed to be punished or have someone else take the punishment for that disobedience and "fall." If God is within us, we cannot be "fallen," and separated from God. Third, Augustine based his theory on the concept of corporate guilt.

Augustine was fluent in Latin, but he was not an excellent Greek scholar. He referred to St. Paul's "Letter to the Romans," 5:12. In it, St. Paul implied something that may have been a metaphor for original sin, but Augustine's interpretation was a mistake that has plagued Christianity ever since. The <u>Jerusalem Bible</u> translates that verse: "Sin entered the world through one man, and through sin, death, and thus death has spread through the whole human race because everyone has sinned." I believe that this is a good paraphrase of Paul's Greek. Paul was using an analogy, which Augustine literalized. Instead of "because everyone has sinned," Augustine translated the Greek into Latin to mean, "in whom all have sinned." The Greek can be ambiguous in that statement, but Augustine made a drastic mistake with some prepositions. That had a huge and tragic influence on Christian doctrine.

As a result of all of this, Augustine won his battle against Pelagius. Now, he believed, that all of humanity is guilty of sin because of shared corporate guilt from Adam and Eve. Humanity now is a "fallen race," that has separated itself from God. Not only has the theory of original sin been based on corporate guilt, but sin was claimed to be passed on through the act of sexual intercourse, something like a venereal disease. This is a horrible notion. It became a basic doctrine of most orthodox Christian theology.

From the traditional Augustinian theory of original sin, and a "fallen" human race which must be redeemed, came the popular Protestant beliefs that every person is a miserable sinner, and deserves to spend eternity in hell because of Adam's sin and also because of personal sins. The followers of John Calvin and some other Protestant theologians of the Reformation built their cases upon this belief. Salvation was possible only for believers in Christ's redemptive sacrifice and atonement. For some, who took the idea as far as "predestination," only those who had been pre-destined by God to obtain salvation before they even were born, could be "saved" from punishment in hell. For the rest, there was little hope. No wonder so many have rejected Christianity!

For Roman Catholics, the story was equally preposterous. For centuries, the Roman Catholic Church held to a doctrine of "limbo," as a place where unbaptized people may spend eternity. It was not purgatory nor hell nor heaven. Eventually, the Roman Catholic Church declared that limbo does not exist. (Finally, they did admit a mistake!)

The author of the "Letter to the Hebrews" (who was not St. Paul,) made it very clear throughout his letter that Jesus Christ was perfect in every way. That belief may be summed up in Hebrews 4:14, in which Christ is designated the great high priest, who has been tempted in every way as we are, yet he is without sin. The early Christian Church emphasized that Jesus was without sin. This raised some theological questions. If Jesus was conceived by the Holy

Spirit, he still was born of a woman, the "virgin" Mary. Since Mary was human, she must have inherited original sin from her parents, even if she herself had lived a sinless life. Therefore, Jesus would have inherited original sin from his mother, Mary. The Roman Catholic Church concluded, therefore, that Mary must have been preserved from inheriting original sin from her parents, Ann and Joachim, at the moment of her conception. That way, Mary later could become the perfect "vessel" to give birth to Jesus without him inheriting original sin from her. This is called the "Immaculate Conception." It refers to Mary's conception, not to Jesus's conception, as many mistakenly think. The Immaculate Conception was proclaimed on December 8, 1854 by Pope Pius IX. It became one of the few dogmas of the Roman Catholic Church. (*Ineffabilis Deus*.) [33]

(More binding than a doctrine, belief in a dogma is considered by the Roman Catholic Church to be necessary for salvation. Is this men playing God?)

Roman Catholic theologians concluded that since Mary did not inherit original sin, and lived her entire life without sin, she should not have had to inherit the punishments stated in "Genesis" 3:14-19 for the original sin of Adam and Eve. Therefore, some Roman Catholics claim that

Mary should not have had to suffer while giving birth to Jesus. Jesus simply passed through Mary's womb like light through glass. (That is not an official doctrine.) Many Roman Catholics believe that Mary's womb remained intact throughout her life, and that she never had sexual intercourse or gave birth to any more children. This is referred to as the "Perpetual Virginity of Mary." Of course, the gospels speak about Jesus's brothers and sisters. This reflects a prevalent attitude that sexual relations somehow are associated with sin.

Finally, since Mary was sinless, her body should not have decayed after her death, as the "Genesis" curse also stated. On November 1, 1950, Pope Pius XII proclaimed the dogma of the Assumption of the Blessed Virgin Mary. (*Munificentissimus Deus.*) This stated that at the time of Mary's death, her physical body was taken "up" into heaven.[34] One might argue that Mary's tomb is believed by some to have been in the Kidron Valley in Jerusalem, where there is a shrine, and by others at a shrine near Ephesus.

Why is all this information about the myth of Adam and Eve, original sin, corporate guilt, the depraved nature of "fallen" humanity and Mariology important? It demonstrates the mistakes of interpreting scripture literally, and of basing theological doctrines on myths. Equally impossible are attempts to explain doctrine as if it were a problem of logic, i.e., "if that is the case, therefore this must be the conclusion." All these questions must remain mysteries, in spite of mankind's desire to have all of the answers. There are no answers. There are only mysteries, which can be partially enlightened through meditation into a realm of the numinous, or mystical.

The Religious Society of Friends rejected theories that mankind is basically evil, "fallen," separated from God and in need of sacrificial redemption. They reacted against Catholicism, Calvinism and Anglicanism. God, the Inner Light, is within every person. God is the Ground of our being. God is both a presence and a power within us. Because of this, humanity is capable of goodness. No one is perfect, but perfection is an ideal to which we all must strive, with the help of God's direct revelation and power within us. Because God is present in every person, there is good in every person, even if it is difficult at times to recognize that goodness. Jesus is our supreme example of how to accept, forgive, support and try to love all persons, in spite of all the negative problems that may separate us. "Nothing can ever come between us and the love of God, made visible in Christ Jesus our Lord." (Romans 8:39.)

Sin: Not Breaking Laws. *Hamartia*

Concern about "sin" seems to be central in any discussion of religion. Because the word "sin" is ambiguous in the scriptures, it often is misunderstood. Throughout much of scripture, the word "sin" has been translated from the Greek word *hamartia*. That Greek word expresses what "sin" really should mean. It does not mean merely breaking laws or rules. The Greek word *hamartia* has to do with targets. It means missing the mark, or "bull's-eye" on a target. If I were to shoot an arrow at a target, and I miss the bull's-eye, that would be *hamartia*. For us, therefore, "sin" means that we have missed the targets of our lives. Those targets represent the ideals, the perfections, the very best that, with God's help, we have the capacity to become the persons that God wills us to become. We see in Jesus a man who lived as the fulfillment of divine ideals. We cannot fully achieve those ideals. We are imperfect. But, the presence of God within us can enable us to strive constantly to live more closely to the targets of our ideals, our potentials. We do not always see the Light of God. But it always is there, enabling us to improve our lives. That enabling power is called God's "grace." The divine Inner Light guides us away from sin. It enlightens and empowers us to do God's will.

An Angry God

Following a Good Friday service, a woman came to my office rather upset. In a somewhat accusatory tone, she demanded, "Don't you believe that Christ died to pay for our sins?" Obviously, she had misunderstood my homily. I explained that I did not accept that Biblical myth as being the best way to express the Atonement. No, I do not believe that Jesus was sacrificed to pay God ("ransom") for our sins.

What I was trying to say was that I reject the idea that Jesus's sacrificial death was necessary in order to pay for the sins of mankind, and therefore to appease an angry, human-like God. The traditional, orthodox doctrine of the Atonement is based on the concept of corporate identity and corporate guilt. If one person sinned, all shared in his or her guilt. But, that guilt could be transferred to another person or to an animal, such as the sacrificial, pascal lamb or a scapegoat. They were sacrificed to pay the price or to atone for the sins of all the people. This concept was applied to Jesus, believing that all of humanity was embodied in his sacrifice. He was the pascal lamb or scapegoat. That metaphor still may be a valid symbol for us, as it was for the ancient Hebrews, but it cannot be taken literally.

The idea that God (or gods) were angry at certain individuals or groups, and had to be appeased, was common among most primitive cultures. In Christianity, those beliefs developed from the myth of the sin of Adam and Eve. Jesus's sacrificial death was to pay God for forgiveness of our sins. A horrible concept!

Medieval theologians such as Saint Anselm (1033-1109) claimed that since mankind had to pay God for the sins of humanity, only a human could pay the price by offering the sacrifice. But, no human was perfect enough to be acceptable to God as a sacrifice for sins except the perfect man, Jesus, God the Son. Jesus was both human and divine. All of this assumes an angry and vengeful God. It fits into the themes of so many universal myths. It is called the "substitutionary" theory of the Atonement. It states that Jesus was sacrificed to God as a "substitute" for each of us to redeem us from sin. I reject that doctrine. My theory of the Atonement resembles that of Peter Abelard's moral influence theory. (Abelard: 1079-1142.) Abelard believed that our experience of Jesus's suffering on a cross influences us to follow his example and teachings. But we are enabled to do so only by God's presence and power within us. Abelard rejected Anselm's theory. Abelard was deemed to be a heretic. Saint Anselm won.

Jesus

"I seek Jesus beyond scripture, beyond creeds, beyond doctrines, beyond dogmas and even beyond religion itself. Only there will our gaze turn to the mystery of God."
The Rt. Rev. John Shelby Spong, Episcopal Bishop of Newark, N.J. Jesus for the Non-religious. [35]

Jesus of Nazareth was not God who came to earth from a mythological place called "heaven" to live in human form for thirty-three years, and then return to a divine, celestial Trinity. He was the man through whom God was fully manifested. Know the man Jesus, and experience the presence of God. "Jesus is the image (icon) of the unseen God." (Colossians 1:15.) "Jesus is the radiant light of God's glory, and the perfect copy of God's nature." (Hebrews 1:3.) Therefore, it may be said that Jesus was both human and divine. Mystically, Jesus could be called "God the Son," but keep it a mystery. Doctrines are insufficient.

Jesus and Universal Myths

When people hear the words "myth" or "legend," many assume that they are merely fictitious stories. Most myths and legends have profound meanings. A myth or legend as used in scripture is a type of parable. It is a story that is created in order to point beyond itself to explain a deeper meaning that otherwise is too difficult to understand. It is an illustration of something else. Myths are not historic events, as we define "history" or "truth." They are, however, the ways that we attempt to explain things that we believe to be true, but are too mysterious for us to articulate in matter-of-fact terminologies. Myths carry us mystically into realms that defy rational definitions. That is the realm of the numinous. Therefore, when discussing matters of faith, the best ways that we can express our beliefs may be through symbols, allegories, myths, legends, rituals, drama, music, art and parables. Myths and legends are important, but we always must look beyond them to discover their meanings. Literal interpretations destroy their purposes.

Myths that are found in various cultures throughout the world also are prevalent in the Hebrew-Christian scriptures. In many cultures, there are stories of great heroes having a god as father and a human mother. There are Egyptian and Greek myths of dying and rising gods. There are creation myths, some from the Near East, which are very similar to the "Genesis" myths, and probably were the basis for them. There are myths about huge floods. The mother earth goddess is found in almost every ancient culture. (Does Jesus's mother Mary fill that role today for Catholics?) Most all religions, primitive or highly organized, are expressed, in part, by myths.

Early Christians took many of these pagan myths and gave them Christian meanings. Symbolic of this is the way that the birth of Jesus became celebrated on the day that pagans had celebrated the birth of their god, Mithras. All Souls day replaced pagan festivals which honored the dead. Many Christian customs still incorporate aspects of pagan festivals. These are common themes in mythologies throughout the entire world. This does not mean that the stories about the birth of Jesus Christ as told by the authors of the gospels have no meaning other than being quaint legends or myths. These legends and myths were told to explain mysteries that otherwise could not be understood. To refer to the stories about Jesus's birth as told in the gospels of "St. Luke" and "St. Matthew" as "myths" does not deny belief that the human Jesus was the unique manifestation of God. But, they are not primarily about a "virgin" giving birth. They illustrate what Christians call the "Incarnation." Because there are pagan myths about dying and rising gods does not mean that the resurrection appearances of Jesus were fictitious. They are mysteries. They are about how Jesus continues to live eternally after his death. Many very similar, ancient myths have been told in unrelated, primitive cultures throughout the world. Many narratives about Jesus in the gospels have universal meanings. These seem to be basic to many diverse religions and to most of humanity.

A distinction must be made here between Jesus and the various mythological characters of many unrelated cultures throughout the world. Was Jesus the fulfillment of all those prehistoric universal myths? Was Jesus unique? Is there a difference between Jesus Christ and the characters in Bulfinch's Mythology? Is Jesus's mother Mary, called *Theotokos* (God-bearer,) any more than a Christian version of the many female goddesses found in almost every culture? No matter how much or how little she was involved in Jesus's adult life, (we do not know,) Mary has become for Roman Catholics the symbolic representative of all of humanity. She symbolically, mystically, expresses the feminine side of creation.

Some people, such as Thomas Jefferson and theologian Rudolf Bultmann have tried to de-mythologize scripture. Myths and legends are necessary to express mysteries that otherwise could not be articulated. Scripture gives us geographical, dated and descriptive contexts for the great people through whom God was especially manifested in Hebrew-Christian history. Scripture offers us pathways to get back to the original personalities and events. But, scripture cannot be interpreted literally or historically. That is one of the many problems with conservative Christianity. It focuses on myths, rather than on their meanings.

Early Jewish followers of Jesus searched the Hebrew scriptures to find parallels between Jesus and the great Hebrew prophets. How could they justify the messiah suffering and dying? A Jew of Jesus's era would have realized what the stories of Jesus's life and death meant by comparing them to "Old Testament" prophesies. There were "Old Testament" legends behind most "New Testament" stories. In order to understand the "New Testament," we need to delve into the "Old Testament" to discover the relationships between "Old Testament" figures, such as Moses, David, Elijah, Elisha, Hosea, Isaiah and many of the other prophets, to understand the parallels with the stories about Jesus's (alleged) words and actions.

"The Gospel According to St. Mark"

Many ancient, so-called "gospels" have been discovered during the past centuries. They were rejected from the "Canon of Scripture" and suppressed by various bishops and councils. I'll concentrate only on the four gospels in scripture.

The author of the gospel called "St. Mark" wrote *circa* 65 C.E. That is the earliest and the shortest of the four gospels. He wrote to a community that already knew about Jesus and was familiar with the Hebrew scriptures. In Mark's gospel, there are no references to Jesus's birth, except to say that he was the "son of Mary, the brother of James, Joset (Joseph), Jude and Simon." (St. Mark 6:3.) It was very unusual for a Jew to be identified as the son of his mother instead of his father. Rather than take this as an implication that Mark knew the legend of Jesus's virginal conception, I see it more as raising the question of who really was Jesus's father. Or, the text could have been changed later, taking Joseph out of the picture to allow for the "virginal conception" legends. That involves huge debates. "St. Mark" begins with the baptism of Jesus. The stories about his temptations in the wilderness follow immediately. Jesus then went to Galilee and began calling his apostles. He went on to Capernaum to continue his healing and teaching ministry.

A great number of Mark's narratives are expressed in mythological terms, such as ghosts, angels and the "Son of Man" coming in clouds. Yet, in Mark's gospel there are no accounts of resurrection appearances. There was an empty tomb and an angel, who told the women that they should report it to Jesus's apostles, and that Jesus had gone to Galilee where they would see him. ("St. Mark" 16:7.) Mark wrote to convince his readers that Jesus was the one who had inaugurated the kingdom of God. Mark began his gospel with the words, "The beginning of the Good News about Jesus Christ, the Son of God." ("St. Mark" 1:1. Jerusalem Bible.) The Jewish followers of Jesus during Mark's era would have understood most of the ancient Hebrew references.

One of Mark's main themes was that the kingdom of God was at hand. "The time has come...and the kingdom of God is close at hand. Repent, and believe the Good News from God." ("St. Mark" 1:15.) What is meant by "the kingdom of God?" It has many meanings.

The gospels tell us that Jesus proclaimed the imminent establishment of the kingdom of God on earth. He was said to have believed also that the kingdom of God already had arrived and was within each believer. The kingdom of God referred to the time when God will establish divine rule and dominance on the earth. It was not about a heavenly experience after death. In many ways, it was thought to mean a political authority. It was about transforming the earth. "The Book of the Prophet Micah" in chapter 4, verses 3-4 expresses the idea of the kingdom of God beautifully:

> He (God) will wield authority over many peoples and arbitrate for mighty nations. They will hammer their swords into plowshares, and their spears into sickles. Nation will not lift sword against nation; there will be no more training for war. Each man will sit under his vine and his fig tree, and no one will trouble him.....

This description of the kingdom of God sounds very much like the words of "Isaiah" 35:1-6, in which the deserts will bloom, the blind will see, and the dumb will sing. the deaf will hear, the lame will leap. Jesus believed that this would happen soon. ("St. Mark" 9:1.) "I tell you solemnly, there are some standing here who will not taste death before they see the kingdom of God come with power." The prophets Elijah and

Malachi announced the coming of the kingdom of God. Mark's gospel begins with the story of John the Baptist as a messenger who proclaimed that all should repent and prepare for the arrival of the kingdom of God. Some thought that John the Baptist was Elijah, risen from the dead. Elijah had been associated with the proclamation of the arrival of the kingdom of God. ("St. Mark" 9:9-13.) Then, after the death of John the Baptist, Jesus came to be recognized as the one who would announce the coming of the kingdom. Later, (it is alleged by the authors of the gospels,) Jesus declared that it had arrived, and he was the sign of its advent. (In "St. Luke" 4:22, Jesus said that it already was being fulfilled.)

Another image of the kingdom of God can be found in "The Book of Daniel," written between 167 and 164 B.C.E. This idea of the kingdom of God was a radical change from previous concepts. Previously, the Hebrews had believed that the kingdom would be established on earth, where life would change and become beautiful under the reign of God. Eventually, however, people became more pessimistic about the possibility of such changes on the earth as they knew it. Life was a horrible struggle, with the Hebrew people constantly living under the submission of foreign rulers. For Daniel, the kingdom of God would be initiated by the "Son of Man," who would reign forever. The title "Son of Man" previously had meant simply, "a man." For Daniel, it meant an apocalyptic figure, who would come from heaven and bring about the end of this sinful world of suffering and injustice. The world as all knew it, would end. There would be judgment of all people, and God would reign eternally on the earth.

Mark used the title "Son of Man" for Jesus many times as being the Christ (messiah,) the one who would initiate the kingdom of God. In the account of Jesus's trial before the high priest, Jesus was asked, "are you the Christ, the Son of the Blessed?" Mark alleged that Jesus responded, "I am…and you will see the Son of Man sitting at the right hand of the Power and coming with the clouds of heaven." ("St. Mark" 14:61-62.)

All of this demonstrates how the author of "The Gospel According to St. Mark" used references to earlier Hebrew prophets, legends and myths to show how Jesus was the fulfillment of these prophecies, and indeed was the messiah, (the Christ,) the Son of Man, the Son of God. The prophesies were expressed in terms that exist in the mystical realms of the numinous, and should be understood as such.

"The Gospel According to St. Matthew"

The author of St. Matthew's gospel was a Jew writing from a Jewish perspective to a Jewish reading audience. Both of the gospels which are called "St. Matthew" and "St. Luke" were written between 75 and 85 C.E. Again, Matthew's gospel compared Jesus to the great leaders and prophets of Hebrew history, trying to convince his Jewish readers that Jesus was the fulfillment of each of them.

Matthew's gospel begins with the ancestry of Jesus. He begins the genealogy with Abraham, often called the father of the Hebrew people. He names many famous people described in the Hebrew scriptures, who would have been known to the Jews. Eventually, the genealogy comes to David, the great king. The list ends with "Joseph the husband of Mary, of her was born Jesus who is called Christ." ("St. Matthew" 1:1-17.) Note that Jesus's ancestry was traced through Joseph.

Matthew's gospel tried to stress the relationship between Jesus and God more than Mark's had done. (Matthew and Luke both had copies of Mark's gospel, as well as the, now lost "Quelle" or "Q Document" of Jesus's sayings.)

Matthew claimed that Jesus was born in Bethlehem, the city of King David. That legend was created to fulfill the prophecy in "Micah" chapter 5:1, "But you, *Ephrathah* (Bethlehem,) the least of the clans of Judah, out of you will be born for me the one who is to rule over Israel." Jesus was called a son of (descendent of) David. Matthew omitted the story, told by Luke, of the announcement by an angel to Mary that she would give birth to a son. Matthew does say that Mary was betrothed to Joseph. Before Mary and Joseph were married, Mary was found to be pregnant. An angel appeared to Joseph in a dream telling him that Mary had conceived by the Holy Spirit. Matthew omitted the story that is told by Luke about the arduous journey to Bethlehem. The mythology of the angels and legends of shepherds' visits also were omitted by Matthew. Somehow, Mary and Joseph got to Bethlehem. Supposedly, Jesus was born there in a stable. Those stories will be discussed next in "The Gospel According to St. Luke." Each legend has a purpose.

Matthew's legend of the visit of the magi is unique to Matthew's gospel. Herod's order to kill all male children under the age of two years was to fulfill a prophecy in "Jeremiah" 31:15, which refers to Rachel weeping for her dead children. (See also "Genesis" 35:19.) Mary and Joseph took

Jesus and fled to Egypt. This legend was to fulfill the prophesy in "Hosea" 11:1, when God supposedly said, "I called my son out of Egypt."

Considering the traveling time of the magi, they would have arrived to visit Jesus when he was about two years old, having followed a star all that time. The family would have been living in Nazareth, (where I believe Jesus had been born.) Of course, this all is fiction. "Isaiah" 60:3 and "Psalms" 72:10-11 both refer to kings coming from the east to worship the "royal son." They were to bring gold, incense and costly gifts. Imagine an entourage of wealthy magi arriving in a small, backwater town with camels, servants and a long line of traveling equipment. Word would have spread for miles around, and have been the talk of the town for years to come. It would have been like a president of the United States entering a "hick" town "off the beaten path," known for its unsophisticated population. That was Nazareth's reputation. In the fourth gospel, the author has Nathanael asking, "Can anything good come out of Nazareth?" ("St. John" 1:42.) The magi's gifts to Jesus, gold, frankincense and myrrh, symboliz- ed that Jesus would be a king, since gold was associated with kingship. He would be a priest, since incense was associated with the priesthood. Myrrh was a symbol of death, foreshadowing his crucifixion. The magi were foreigners, symbolizing that Jesus was Lord of all people, universally, and not only of the Jews. "St. Matthew" is the only gospel that tells the legend of the magi. None of these legends possibly could be true. But, we do not read scripture for historic truth.

The author of "St. Matthew" wrote that at his baptism Jesus was declared by a voice from heaven to be the Son of God. Next, Jesus spent forty days in the wilderness, being tempted. This is a comparison of the forty years that the Hebrew people spent wondering in the desert before they reached the "Promised Land." (For the Hebrews, certain numbers were considered special. These were three, seven, ten, twelve and forty. They often were used to designate certain periods of time, but those periods of time were not necessarily consistent with the numbers. Usually, they were exaggerations.) "St. Matthew," chapter five, is called "The Sermon on the Mount." It is not a single sermon delivered at one time or place. Rather, it is a combination of many sayings that the author believed that Jesus might have said at one time or another. In verse 17, Jesus is reputed to have said, "Do not think that I have come to abolish the Law or the Prophets." Here it seems that Jesus was setting himself up as the fulfillment of the Law and the Prophets. Of course, these may

154

have been words imagined by the author of the gospel, and not the words of Jesus.

Among the greatest figures of Hebrew history, certainly Moses, David, Elijah, Elisha and Ezekiel all ranked at the top. In "St. Matthew" 22:43, the author raises Jesus even above (King) David, saying, "David, moved by the Spirit, calls him (Jesus) Lord." (The name "David" simply means "beloved, chieftain" or "king." When the Bible speaks about King David, it refers to a king named "Elhanan.") The story of Jesus feeding a huge crowd of more than 5000 followers as told in "St. Matthew" 14:13-21 was reminiscent of Moses and Elijah, who miraculously fed great crowds when their food supply had run out.

Elijah and his successor Elisha were famous for having performed numerous miracles. Jesus was compared to them constantly in the minds of his followers. Consider the story of Jesus's Transfiguration, told in "St. Matthew" and "St. Luke." ("St. Matthew" 17:1-8.) This story most certainly is associated with a mystical experience. Jesus took Peter, James and John up to a high mountain. (Any story which takes place on a high mountain would be reminiscent of Moses on Mt. Sinai. Moses was overwhelmed by an intense light, the presence of God.) Suddenly, on the mountain,

155

Jesus's face shone as intensely as the brightest sunlight. He appeared to be dazzling white. Then, Moses and Elijah appeared. Soon, a cloud enveloped them, and Moses and Elijah disappeared. Only Jesus was left. Peter wanted to build three tents or shrines, so that the vision could be captured and last. (Mystical experiences are transient. They cannot be captured or explained or enshrined.) One obvious point of the story is that Jesus now replaced Moses, who represented the law, and Elijah, who represented the prophets. When Elijah grew old, he did not die. He was believed to have been carried into heaven in a chariot pulled by fiery horses, with a great whirlwind that led him to God above the sky. ("Second Kings" 2-12.) Ezekiel also had a mystical vision of a chariot of fire and the throne of God, which became a very common symbol in Jewish mysticism. Jesus's appearances after his crucifixion and the legend of his ascension into heaven recalled this vision of Elijah. In "St. Matthew" 17:11-12, Jesus was alleged to have said, "Elijah is to come to see that everything is once more as it should be; however, I tell you that Elijah had come already, and they did not recognize him, but treated him as they pleased; and the Son of Man will suffer similarly at their hands." This was referring to John the Baptist, and also was a foreshadowing of Jesus's death.

"The Gospel According to St. Matthew" has other sections unique to that gospel. They often are called the "M Source." They dwell on what seems, at times, to be an obsession for the author of "St. Matthew." They foretell judgment and punishment. In the parable of the good and bad seed, the author wrote that Jesus said, "The Son of Man will send his angels, and they will gather out of his kingdom all things that provoke offenses and all who do evil, and throw them into the blazing furnace, where there will be weeping and grinding of teeth. Then the virtuous will shine like the sun in the kingdom of their father." ("St. Matthew" 13:24-30 and 36-43.)

Many theologians believe that the author of Matthew's gospel was influenced by other middle-eastern religions which dwelt on beliefs of judgment and eternal punishment in a fiery "hell." Personally, I do not believe that Jesus was so obsessed with that belief, although it was part of the prophesies foretelling judgment, punishment and reward. These appear mostly in Matthew's gospel. Hell is a mythical invention which has plagued Christianity throughout the ages. It has filled some believers' lives with guilt and fear every time they think that they are not living up to God's demands. There is some truth to the saying that very often religion does more harm than good.

"The Gospel According to St. Luke"

"The Gospel According to St. Luke" and "The Book of the Acts of the Apostles" were written by the same author. He wrote between 75 and 85 C.E. The author was a well-educated gentile, perhaps a physician from Greece. He was writing to a Hellenistic audience. Some were Jews who had migrated to Greece or Asia Minor. Most were gentile converts to Christianity.

Unique to Luke's gospel are the stories about Mary's visit to Elizabeth, her kinswoman and the mother of John the Baptist. Also, unique to Luke are details regarding the familiar legends of Jesus's birth in Bethlehem. ("St. Luke" 2:1-20.)

I do not want to spoil anyone's Christmas. I do, however, want to urge Christians to delve beyond the legends to understand their purposes. I always began my Christmas sermons by saying that the so-called "nativity stories" that we read in the gospels of Matthew and Luke are entirely mythological and legendary. But, those legends developed for many reasons. We always need to ask, what did they mean to the early Christians when they first were created, and what do they mean for us today? Many Christians today remain stuck in the legends, portrayed in pageants, greeting cards, hymns, nativity scenes and so on, but they do not go beyond those familiar expressions which are so much a part of our culture. For example, we may love to sing Handel's "Messiah," about Isaiah's prophesies, but the prophecies made by Isaiah in the eighth century B.C.E. had nothing to do with the birth of Jesus. No "Old Testament" prophecies can be linked to the actual birth of Jesus. "Isaiah" 9:6-7 foretells the birth of a king of Israel. That refers to King Hezekiah who ruled during the eighth century B.C.E. It docs not refer to Jesus, who was born many centuries later. A great amount of tradition and sentimentality is part of our celebrations of Christmas. These are fine in their place, as legends and myths. I think that one reason why Christmas has become more a secular holiday than a religious observance is because people focus only on the myths and legends, which are no more believable than Santa Claus.

We begin with the Annunciation, ("St. Luke" 1: 26-38,) which says that the angel Gabriel came to Mary and told her that she was to give birth to a son, who would be called the "Son of God." First, I would consider this a myth, because angels are mythological creatures, although some might interpret those visions as mystical revelations.

Second, was Mary a "virgin" as one who never has had sexual intercourse? The word in Greek that is translated as "virgin" has nothing to do with being sexually chaste, as the word "virgin" is used today. It means simply "a young woman."

Mary was engaged to Joseph, but not yet married. Why would the author of "St. Luke" have said that she was pregnant before their marriage? That legend was necessary to explain that Jesus had a human mother but a divine father, God the Holy Spirit. Therefore, Jesus was the God-man. (Olympian mythology?) Some later rumors even said that Mary had been impregnated by a Roman soldier named Panthera. They probably were spread to discredit Christianity. Or was there some embarrassing question about Jesus's paternity? We may ask why these questions and legends about Jesus's conception arose. No one knows.

In college, my Unitarian religion professor had presented the possibility that Jesus's mother might have been raped, and all the legends that had developed about his birth were to cover up that horrible incident. My professor said that it would make a beautiful story if the man who was believed to have been the supreme expression of divine love, had such a background. When I heard that in class, I became angry, in spite of my respect for my professor. But, for me today, such a story would not diminish my belief in Jesus as being the fully human man, who uniquely manifested God's love. Let it remain a mystery.

The author of Luke's gospel had his dates incorrect. He was a Greek, who probably was not well informed about Jewish history. Quirinius became governor of Syria only in the year 6 C.E., probably at least two years after Jesus's birth. He did conduct a census of Judea for tax purposes, but there is no record of an earlier census. Moreover, the Roman system of taxation did not require one to return to one's place of birth or family origin. Property was taxed at its location. Also, Mary would not have been required to accompany Joseph. Therefore, Joseph and Mary would not have had to travel to Bethlehem. In the gospels of both Luke and Matthew, the stories of Mary and Joseph traveling to Bethlehem were invented to make people believe that Jesus was born in Bethlehem as foretold in Hebrew prophesies. Joseph's lineage was traced back to King David. (Notice that it was through Joseph's lineage, not Mary's.) Bethlehem was called the "city of David." Therefore, Jesus must be a descendent or "son of David." But, Jesus came from Nazareth, where he probably was born. Herod died in 4 B.C.E. His son, Archelaus reigned in Judea after him.

"St. Luke" tells the stories of angels and shepherds visiting the infant Jesus in Bethlehem. Then the family returned to Nazareth. "St. Luke" does not mention the visit of the magi or the family's flight into Egypt. He goes on to tell of Jesus's circumcision and presentation in the temple. The next story in Luke's gospel tells of Jesus at age twelve going on a pilgrimage with his parents to Jerusalem for the feast of the Passover. Jesus had become separated from his parents, and after much frantic searching for him, they found him in the temple discussing the Hebrew law with theologians. (I do not believe that Jesus ever had superhuman knowledge. He was exceptionally, perhaps uniquely perceptive, but his knowledge was limited to his human condition. See Philippians 2:6-11. Charles Gore's Kenotic theory stated that Jesus abandoned his attributes of deity, such as omniscience and omnipotence.)

It soon becomes obvious that the "Christmas stories" were composed by Matthew and Luke to try to prove that Jesus was the fulfillment of the "Old Testament" prophesies. They were attempts to claim that he was the messiah, a descendent of David, and the Son of God. These stories about Jesus's birth are not found in any of the other books of the "New Testament." Does this mean that we should dismiss all the legends in scripture as fiction? Absolutely not. But, we need to contemplate each of them through the mystical lens of the numinous realm to discover why they were created, and what they were intended to express. We remember stories more than doctrines.

Many of the stories about Jesus in the gospels assume that he was divine, God Incarnate. That belief came only after Jesus's resurrection appearances. Any statements that refer to his divinity were written into the gospels decades later. I do not believe that Jesus or any of his followers ever thought of him as divine. That would have been unthinkable for a Jew. Doubtless, Jesus thought of himself as a healer and a prophet, predicting the end of the current evil age and of a future king of Israel who would rule in an age to come. Whether or not he ever thought of himself as being the messiah, is a question. He supposedly said, many times, that the kingdom of God had come, and that people were experiencing it at that present time. In "St. Luke" 4:18-19, 21, at the beginning of his public ministry, Jesus went into the synagogue in Nazareth on the Sabbath day, and stood up to read. He read from the prophet "Isaiah" 61:1-2. "The spirit of the Lord has been given to me, for he has anointed me, He has sent me to bring the good news to the poor, to proclaim liberty to captives, and to the blind, new sight, to

163

set the downtrodden free, and to proclaim the Lord's year of favor." Then, according to Luke's rendition, Jesus said, "This text is being fulfilled today even as you listen." Here, it would seem, that Jesus was implying that he was the messiah, and that the kingdom of God already was present. That incident enraged those who were listening to Jesus in the synagogue. The crowd ran Jesus out of town, and threatened to throw him down a cliff, but he slipped away from them.

Probably at some time during Jesus's ministry, his followers began to think of him as the messiah. For many Jews of Jesus's era, there were expectations of two messiahs, one a political and military leader who would drive out the Roman oppressors, and the other, a spiritual prophet who would purify the Jewish religion and establish a new kingdom under God's rule. How did Jesus fit those expectations? I agree with many "New Testament" scholars that it could have been only after his followers believed that he was alive and present with them after his crucifixion that they would have begun to think of him as divine. That thought would have taken years to develop. We first find it expressed in the letters written by St. Paul after 49 C.E. St. Paul was the earliest writer to develop a detailed Christology. Jesus would have been shocked by Paul's theories!

"The Gospel According to St. John"

"The Gospel According to St. John" (the fourth gospel) was written around 110 C.E., by someone who was part of a group of Christians that identified themselves with the apostle John. The "Book of Revelation" (*Apocalypse*) may have been written by the same group. The apostle John had lived in Ephesus. He died around the year 98 C.E. Tradition says that John had cared for Jesus's mother Mary after Jesus's death. Mary's tomb near Ephesus became a very popular shrine for some Christians.

Bishop John Shelby Spong wrote in his book Eternal Life: "A New Vision," that it is "through a mystical lens" that we can understand John's gospel.[36] The faith of the author of the fourth gospel was firmly within the numinous realm. It was mystical. Bishop Spong wrote, "The story of Jesus is not of a divine life invading the world, but of a human life named Jesus of Nazareth." Bishop Spong continued, "Yet, the gospel portrays this Jesus as revealing a deeper and freer self-consciousness that is so profound that the usual human barriers disappeared: John portrays Jesus as having a relationship with the holy that is of indistinguishable identity."[37] When we see Jesus through the lens of mysticism, in the realm of the numinous, we can better understand what the writer of the fourth gospel was trying to demonstrate in the "I am" statements.

Did Jesus actually make the "I am" statements in chapters five through ten of the fourth gospel? Most "New Testament" scholars agree that he did not. I do not think that Jesus ever believed or said such things about himself. The author of the gospel created those statements to show how he believed that Jesus replaced the various celebrations of the Hebrew liturgical calendar. Through this literary composition, Jesus then "becomes" the fulfillment of each Jewish event or symbol of faith as they were observed throughout each year. He replaces the law by healing on the Sabbath. He becomes the bread of life by feeding the crowds of 5000. The Passover bread and wine become his body and blood. In "St. John," Jesus died on the day that the Passover lambs were slaughtered. His torn flesh and blood on the cross replace the sacrificial Passover lamb. Jesus becomes the vine and wine. He becomes living water and the light of the world fulfilling the Feasts of Tabernacles, Hanukkah and Dedications. He is the shepherd at the door. Jesus becomes the new temple to be destroyed and raised up in three days. Jesus becomes the fulfillment of Elijah, the prophets, and the laws in the Torah. He was reputed to have said, "I am," to each of these. These statements were literary devices, composed long after Jesus's death and resurrection appearances. The readers of the fourth gospel, being familiar with the Hebrew scriptures and liturgical calendar, would have recognized the symbolism in each of these statements. Statements attributed to Jesus in the fourth gospel, such as, "Before Abraham was, I am," or, "The one who has seen me has seen the Father," or, "The Father and I are one," all were created by the author to try to prove to his readers that Jesus not only was the fulfillment of all the Hebrew heroes, prophesies and events, but he also was the manifestation of God. That is mystical.

The statement "I AM" was used as an identity by God in the "Old Testament." In "Exodus" 3:14, God says to Moses, "I AM WHO I AM." Later Christians would have understood how the author of the gospel was attempting to identify Jesus with God. If Jesus actually had used those words, everyone would have considered them blasphemous. He would have been identifying himself as God, a crime always punishable by execution. I believe that Jesus was crucified for political crimes more than religious, although the Jews made no distinction between political and religious. He was a threat to both authorities.

The Letters of Saint Paul

Although Saint Paul never saw or heard Jesus while Jesus lived, Paul stamped his own interpretation upon Jesus more than any other writer in the "New Testament." Paul's relationship with Jesus was completely mystical, in the sacred, numinous realm.

Paul, a Hellenized Jew, originally known as Saul of Tarsus, was involved in persecutions of Christians, including the stoning of St. Stephen. While on a journey to Damascus, Paul suddenly was struck by a blinding light. He fell to the ground, and heard a voice saying, "Saul, Saul, why are you persecuting me...? I am Jesus, and you are persecuting me." ("Acts" 9:3-6.) Saul changed his name to Paul, and drastically changed his entire attitude about Jesus and Christianity. He became the liberal voice of Jewish converts to early Christianity, opposing the strict, legalistic, orthodox Jews, especially those who held high, powerful positions in the Jerusalem temple.

Saint Paul was very well acquainted with Hebrew scriptures, symbols and practices. Paul saw Jesus as the fulfillment of the Hebrew scriptures. He would have been familiar with the image in "Isaiah" 40-55 of the "suffering servant," which was applied to Jesus. He would have observed the Day of Atonement, and the Passover, when animals were sacrificed for the sins of the Hebrew people. Paul applied the same imagery to Jesus's death, as a sacrifice to God for human sins.

In his "Letter to the Philippians" Paul wrote that Jesus was eternally divine and equal to God. But Jesus did not cling to his equality with God. (Readers would have compared Jesus with Adam and Lucifer, who both wanted to be equal to God.) Paul said that Jesus "emptied himself" of all divine powers, (omnipotence, omniscience etc.) He became a man as all men are, even a slave. ("Philippians" 2:6-8.) In "First Corinthians" 15, Paul compared Jesus with Adam. Christ became the new man, not born of earth, perishable and corrupt, but a man of heaven.

Paul wrote about Jesus's resurrection as appearances of a "glorified body," and not a resuscitated corpse. (See later chapters.) In his mind, Paul must have compared the imagery of Elijah in "Second Kings" with Jesus's resurrection. Elijah was carried to heaven in a fiery chariot.

Continuous Revelation

During the first few centuries of the early Christian Church, many different Christian sects arose around the known world. Some of these were deemed heretical by Church Councils. Many of these groups had produced their own written versions of Christianity in what they called "gospels." Eventually, councils of bishops and theologians settled on a certain list of books from the "Old Testament." Then they considered the many writings about Jesus and the Christian faith that had become popular. They rejected some, most of which were forbidden and destroyed, and they accepted others, our present-day scriptures.

Among conservative Protestants, there arose a belief that the <u>Bible</u> as we know it, contains "all things necessary for salvation." In other words, when the "Canon of Scripture," was closed, they believed that it contained completely all divine revelation. Nothing could be added to it. Roman Catholics reject that theory, believing that the Catholic Church continues to interpret revelation. Most liberal Christians today believe that the Holy Spirit continues to reveal the will of God. Those who believe in direct revelation agree. Revelation continues to evolve.

Christians and Others

My critical discussions regarding scripture and doctrines cannot be interpreted to mean that it is not necessary for Christians to study scripture and theology. I am objecting to a literal interpretation of scripture and a dogmatic authority defining doctrines. Christians need to know scripture as our focus for meditations and direct revelations. During meditation, I usually try to focus on my revelations concerning Jesus Christ, but I often focus also on thoughts from other faith traditions, and on many of the people whom I regard as my "heroes," those who have made the world a better place, especially through non-violent methods. Consider Mohandas Gandhi.

All persons will envision, imagine, understand and experience their faith in very different, personal and individual ways. This leads me to the conclusion that all faith experiences must be seen as subjective and relative. No one can claim absolute or universal truth in matters of faith or revelation. I do not believe that Jesus ever said, "No one can come to the Father except through me." Those words were invented by the author of the fourth Gospel in his attempt to convert others, and to "market" Christianity as the only true faith.

There are many Christians who will claim that some of the accounts in scripture that I consider to be legends, for them, are very true, literally and historically. They are necessary expressions of their faith. Other people may question many of the accounts that I believe are helpful to my faith. We all may differ in how we interpret our faith. Faith comes from experience.

While visiting some churches, I might recite the Nicene Creed or the "Hail Mary." Perhaps in a mystical way, these might express something about my own faith, even if I do not believe them literally. They are in another realm of consciousness, the numinous. Doubtless, Buddhists, Hindus, Jews, Muslims, Celts, Native Americans and others of numerous different faith traditions believe that the mystical experiences that they have encountered have been direct revelations from their concepts of the divine. I often receive great inspiration from each of those non-Christian faiths. They too, reveal the Inner Light!

I believe that God is in all people and faiths. I experience God mostly through my concepts of Jesus Christ. Others will have different experiences. But somehow, we all are related to the one God. We all are joined to each other in one divine Existence that has many names and faces.

Doctrine

Faith must be based on experience rather than on scripture and doctrines. But, scripture and theological theories may help to provide a context for faith. Doctrines and creeds, however, are nothing more than human, theological theories. They are not absolutes.

Doctrines and creeds reduce the mysteries of faith to human terminologies. They create a "god" in the image of mankind, and then attempt to apply logic to that image to construct theological definitions. Faith cannot be dissected. It cannot be approached like a mathematical problem, theorizing that if one proposition is true, therefore another must be true. That is human logic, not faith. Faith is not a logical system.

"Creeds and doctrines bind people to the faith experiences of others, not of their own. They stifle direct revelations and restrict new revelations from God. They are static, limited to the theological and political prejudices of religious leaders. They become authorities in and of themselves, excluding those who do not accept them." [38]

The Nicene Creed
Issued in 325 C.E., Council of Nicaea

The Nicene Creed, as printed in the <u>Book of Common Prayer</u> of the Episcopal Church of the United States of America, 1979. "Holy Eucharist," Rite I. Pages 327-328.

I believe in one God, the Father Almighty, maker of heaven and earth, and of all things visible and invisible,

And in one Lord, Jesus Christ, the only-begotten Son of God, begotten of his Father before all worlds, God of God, Light of Light, very God of very God, begotten, not made, being of one substance with the Father, by whom all things were made; who for us men and for our salvation came down from heaven, and was incarnate by the Holy Ghost (Spirit) of the Virgin Mary, and was made man; and was crucified also for us under Pontius Pilate; he suffered and was buried; and on the third day he rose again according to the scriptures, and ascended into heaven, and sitteth on the right hand of the Father; and he shall come again, with glory, to judge the quick and the dead; whose kingdom shall have no end.

And I believe in the Holy Ghost (Spirit,) the Lord, and Giver of Life, who preceedeth from the Father and the Son, who with the Father and the Son together is worshipped and glorified; who spake by the prophets.

And I believe in one holy Catholic and Apostolic Church; I acknowledge one Baptism for the remission of sins; and I look for the resurrection of the dead, and the life of the world to come. Amen.

(See also: The Apostles' Creed, found on pages 53 and 54, and The Creed of Saint Athanasius, on pages 864 and 865 of the 1979 Book of Common Prayer of the Episcopal Church of the U.S.A.)

From the Council of Chalcedon, 451, Act V. (Excerpts)

Our Lord Jesus Christ, Son, Lord, at once complete in Godhead and complete in manhood, truly God and truly man, consisting also of a reasonable soul and body; of one substance (*homoousios*) with the Father as regards to his Godhead, and at the same time with one substance with us as regards his manhood, like us in all respects, apart from sin..., recognized in two natures..., the distinction of natures being in no way annulled by the union, but rather the characteristics of each nature being preserved and coming together to form one person and substance, not parted or separated into two persons, but one and the same Son and Only-begotten God the Word, Lord Jesus Christ....

From the 1979 Book of Common Prayer, Page 864.

Doctrine

Most scholars admit that the pictures of Jesus that are portrayed in the "New Testament" and by the Church Councils, are very different from the historical Jesus. In Christianity as we know it today, the Christ of the Church probably has very little resemblance to the historical Jesus.

The Incarnation

When I read, or in the past have tried to teach what theologians throughout the ages have said about Jesus, I often disagree with most of their books, creeds and doctrines. They have buried the humanity of Jesus under a pile of mythological divinity, removing Jesus from the world of human reality. Roman Catholics have done the same thing to Jesus's mother, Mary. Popular piety among some Roman Catholics has obscured the humanity of Mary also, turning her into a goddess. It all is unfortunate and frustrating!

Traditional definitions of the Incarnation are extremely complex and confusing. They presuppose a Triune God as one God. God is expressed as three "persons," Father, Son and Holy Spirit. These are descriptions of three ways that mankind has experienced God. They state that the Triune God has existed eternally, from before all creation. This one God, in three divine persons, dwells "in heaven," above the earth. God the Son, (also called the "Logos,") while remaining fully divine, "came down from heaven" to live as a man, Jesus of Nazareth. Jesus was conceived by God the Holy Spirit and a young woman (called a "virgin") named Mary. Jesus was both fully divine and fully human. He lived a perfect, sinless human life, but was unjustly crucified for blasphemy. His sacrificial death on a cross enabled the salvation of mankind by paying God for the sins (original and actual) of all of humanity (or, as some claim, only for the redemption of the predestined or of baptized believers.) Jesus was raised from death and appeared to many of his followers. Forty days after his resurrection, he was elevated back into heaven, where he lives with God the Father and God the Holy Spirit as one God, the Holy Trinity.

I believe that this theology presents confusing symbolism, even though it remains the orthodox and traditional explanation of who Jesus was and his relationship to God. A question that my students often asked was how did the Trinity remain the Trinity while God the Son was on the earth living as Jesus. Also, did Jesus pay only God the Father for mankind's sins? Good questions.

177

In "Philippians," 2:6-11, Saint Paul wrote about Jesus:

His state was divine, yet he did not cling to his equality with God, but emptied himself to assume the condition of a slave, and became man as men are. He was humbler yet, even to accepting death, death on a cross. But God raised him high and gave him the name which is above all other names, that all beings in the heavens, on the earth and in the underworld, should bend the knee at the name of Jesus, and that every tongue should acclaim Jesus as Lord, to the glory of God the Father.

The author of the fourth gospel ("St. John") expressed the Incarnation differently in his prologue to the gospel. Here, "Logos" is translated as "Word," referring to Jesus, as the eternal, pre-existing creator, God the Son:

In the beginning was the Word, The Word was with God and the Word was God. He was with God in the beginning. Through him all things came to be. Not one thing had its being but through him. All that came to be, had life in him, and that light shines in the dark, a light that darkness could not overpower.... The Word was the true light that enlightens all men; and he was coming into the world. He was in the world that had its being through him, and the world did not know him. He came into his own domain, and his own people did not accept him. But to all who did accept him he gave power to become children of God.... The Word was made flesh, and lived among us, and we saw his glory, the glory that is his as the only Son of the Father, full of grace and truth.   (Jerusalem Bible.)

The Oxford Dictionary of the Christian Church defines the "Incarnation" as the doctrine that, "affirms that the eternal Son of God took human flesh from his mother, and the historical Christ is at once fully God and fully man." [39]

These explanations of the Incarnation of God the Son taking on the human flesh of Jesus, are found in many places throughout the "New Testament" in various expressions, but all refer to God becoming a man in Jesus Christ. They are repeated in each of the three Christian creeds. This all sounds like Olympian mythology. In many ancient Greek myths, some great heroes had a god as their father and a (human) woman as their mother. The problem is that among most Christians, this has been taken literally, and not as a myth or metaphor or parable. Here is an excellent

179

example of why one must view doctrine from the mystical, numinous realm, but not as intricate, literal definitions. The Christian creeds are ancient, mythological attempts to define a mystery. Respect them for what they are, myths.

The Rt. Rev'd. John A.T. Robinson wrote in his book Honest to God, "But suppose the whole notion of 'a God' who visits the earth in the person of 'his Son' is as mythical as the prince in a fairy story? Suppose there is no realm 'out there' from which the 'man from heaven' arrives?" [40] Bishop Robinson went on to quote John Wren-Lewis, "The commonest vision of Jesus was not as a human being at all. He was a God in human form, full of supernatural knowledge and miraculous power, very much like the Olympian gods were supposed to be when they visited the earth in disguise."[41] Dr. Paul Tillich, in his Systematic Theology, "Volume Two," (p. 161,) wrote, "The Christological dogma saved the Church, but with very inadequate conceptual tools." [42]

Let's look at Jesus's divinity from a different point of view. I refer to such theologians as Paul Tillich, Bishop John A.T. Robinson and Bishop John Shelby Spong. I express my belief in Jesus's divinity by saying that "Jesus was the man through whom God uniquely was perfectly manifested." (Spong.) "Jesus is the image of the unseen God." (Colossians 1:15.) Those statements satisfy my questions concerning Christology. Beyond that, I leave it to mystery and faith.

Bishop John A.T. Robinson discussed the Greek words used by the author of "The Gospel According to St. John." The Greek in "St. John" 1:14 says, *Kai theos en ho logos.* That usually has been translated, "The Word ('Logos') was made flesh." Robinson wrote that the Greek really said, "And what God was, the Word was." (The Word, or "Logos," refers to Jesus Christ.) Robinson wrote, "In other words, if one looked at Jesus, one saw God." (In "St. John" 14:9, Jesus is supposed to have said, "He who has seen me has seen the Father.") Robinson continued, "Jesus was the complete expression, the Word, (Logos) of God. Through him, as through no one else, God spoke and God acted. When one met him one was met, and saved and judged, by God. And it was to this conviction the apostles bore their witness.... Christ was a window into God at work." [43]

If one takes seriously the theology of Paul Tillich and those who have espoused his theories, (Bishops Robinson, Spong and many others,) then one cannot imagine a God somewhere "in the sky" removed from humanity. Paul Tillich described

God as "the Ground of our Being." Bishop Spong describes God as "Existence" itself, and yet greater than all existence. These theories reflect the definitions of panentheism. If this is true, then God is not separate from us, and we are not separate from God, although God is all of Existence. I repeat and maintain my understanding of the Incarnation, that Jesus was fully man, who throughout his human life, completely and perfectly manifested God. (Bishop Spong.) I do not think that anything more can be said. Beyond that, the Incarnation is a mystery. So be it.

For me, this is the best approach to the mysteries of the Incarnation. It is completely consistent with the Quaker belief that God is the "Inner Light" within every person regardless of religion or faith. God was in Jesus as the perfect and complete "Inner Light" that was not hidden or distorted by sin. When we see, hear or experience the man Jesus, we see, hear and experience God. Another way of stating this, as expressed by Bishop Spong, is to say that God is "Existence" itself. We all are part of Existence, and Existence is part of us. Jesus, uniquely, was at one with Existence (God.) The emphasis must be on the fact that Jesus of Nazareth was fully human, a man, not God in human form or disguise. We see God through Jesus's humanity, his human life, not through his divinity. The Quaker concept of the "Inner Light," and Bishop John Shelby Spong's concept of "Existence," both point us to God. [44]

C.S. Lewis, in his "Essay Collection: Faith, Christianity and the Church," wrote, "The heart of Christianity is a myth which also is a fact. The old myth is of the dying God...who comes down from the heaven of legend and imagination to the earth of history." Then Lewis went on to write, "In the Christian story, myth becomes fact." [45] That is the important point. We hear the myths, and understand them to be myths, but through faith, those myths lead us to our basic Christian beliefs. They lead us beyond mere reason to what cannot be defined. It only can be experienced. Faith is found in the numinous realm. It is mystical.

Whenever there is controversy, as there certainly was in the early Church, people tend to exaggerate their views to overcompensate against those in opposition. This became obvious in the early debates about Christology. If and how was Jesus human or divine or both? Some over-empathized his divinity, others his humanity. The pendulum swung back and forth.

Most Christians believe that Jesus was divine as well as human. Of course, other than through mythology, the "God-man" is impossible to define. Still, the leaders of the early Christian Church wanted definitions, explanations, answers that would satisfy human reason spelled out in human terms. They approached Christology as if it were a mathematical or logic problem. "If this is the case, therefore that must follow." They literalized the myths, and Christians have been confused ever since. They fiercely defended those man-made explanations, which presuppose a three-storied universe, with heaven above the earth as a place where God, a celestial, divine person, resides. The result to this day has been that the man Jesus of Nazareth has been elevated more and more into the realm of the divine, with divinity overshadowing his humanity by far. That has completely obliterated the belief that Jesus was a man, who uniquely manifested the love of God. It is based on mythological concepts that no rational person today could believe outside of the theological metaphors. I am proposing a very different theological base from traditional, orthodox definitions. The differences appear to be subtle, but they are not. The manifestation of God must be seen through the perfect and fullest humanity of the man Jesus.

(This was emphasized by Bishop John S. Spong in his book, Eternal Life: "A New Vision.") [46]

184

As previously stated, Christian doctrines and the three creeds assume that the Triune God "dwells" somewhere beyond and separate from humanity and the world. Perhaps I am guilty of stressing the imminence of God, as I emphasize the belief that God is within every person. But, for me, to say that the eternal and preexisting God the Son, came "down from heaven" and was incarnate in Jesus Christ, makes no sense. God is not "up in heaven." That is ancient mythology. God is within every human being and in all existence.

Of course, my approach to theology and Christology invalidates literal beliefs in the Annunciation, the virginal conception of Jesus, the "nativity narratives," the bodily resurrection, and the ascension of Jesus back to his Father in heaven. My views question the creedal statements that Jesus existed from before all time, and was the creator of all that exists. Those theories do not need to be in my theological scheme of faith. They all may be imagined mystically, but never literally. Jesus was a man, born of a human man and woman, who, as a man, was the perfect manifestation of God, the human image of God. That is different from the statements in the creeds. It does, however, affirm my belief that when we mystically know Jesus, we experience God.

Considering the second coming of Christ, when the liturgy of the Eucharist states, "Christ will come again," I quietly add, "Christ *has* come again." Christ is present now, just as he was to his followers after his crucifixion, to St. Paul at his conversion, and to all humanity ever since. And yes, he will come again and again, always, eternally! Christ is alive. He is the Inner Light in every human being. Jesus told his followers that they could do all the miracles that he did, because God dwells in everyone, just as God dwelt completely in him. (See "St. John" 14:12.)

People often ask me if I am a Unitarian. Most Unitarians approach religion (or agnosticism) from a rational point of view. My faith, with Quakers and many others, arises from mysticism. I agree with Unitarians in many ways. With Unitarians, I agree that faith should not be expressed in intricate, complex doctrines and creeds. Many people want the security of explanations and answers to their questions about God, life and death. I agree that there are no definite answers to these mysteries. I agree also that we should be concerned more with what happens in this life than with theories about the "hereafter." Many Unitarians, however, have drifted away from Christianity. My faith is centered on the man Jesus, as I know him through direct revelation.

Early Heresies

During the first few centuries of the early Church, many Christian communities grew up throughout the vast Roman empire. Some of these groups had little contact with other followers of Jesus. Each group developed its own way of understanding Jesus, its own theology. Many wrote their own "gospels" about how they imagined Jesus had lived and taught. Often, these various interpretations were extremely different.

Around the end of the second century, a belief called "Gnosticism" became very popular among Christians. Gnosticism had many forms. It is too complex to describe here. Basically, the Gnostics believed that a special *gnosis* or secret knowledge of God had been given to the apostles and to other individuals by direct revelation. (Some Christians criticize mysticism as being Gnostic because of its emphasis on direct revelation. I do not agree. The concepts are very different. Direct revelation is not "secret" knowledge.) One form of Gnosticism involved a "demiurge," a creator god who was a remote, divine being. Jesus was sent by God as the "representative" of God. Jesus was a divine being who did not totally assume human form, but temporarily seemed to inhabit a human body, and merely appeared to be human. He did not die, but just appeared to do so, because God could not die. Most of these ideas came from Greek dualism. They believed that the human body was evil. God, therefore, could not have been contaminated by entering a human body. Therefore, God merely appeared to be human. This overemphasized the divinity of Jesus, and made it impossible for him to have been human, in "evil" flesh.

When discussing Christology, (the relationship between God and Christ,) two technical terms must be defined. These are "person" and "nature." "Nature" means any aspect of a being that can be described, such as one's body, mind, will, personality and physical characteristics. That includes what we perceive through our senses and understanding. "Person" refers to one's entire being, including his or her nature. This can mean the ego, the self, the one who acts through his or her nature. One's "person" cannot be described, except to say that he or she exists, acts, and experiences through his or her nature. [47] The Church teaches that Christ is one person, God the Son, acting through two distinct and two complete natures, human and divine.[48] That definition took decades to be articulated, understood and accepted. More heresies and conflicts developed. (See page 175, "Council of Chalcedon.")

From Gnosticism, the theological, Hegelian pendulum swung back to the other side. This dialectic promoted a theory held by Sabellius, a theologian in Rome who taught from 198 to 217 C.E. He emphasized the Hebrew belief that there is only one God. Although Saballius recognized three expressions of God, Father, Son and Holy Spirit, he taught that the one God merely is revealed in three different ways at different times, but they all are the same person. [49] This led to confusion over which person of the Trinity died on the cross. Was it God the Son, Jesus? Or did God the Father and the Holy Spirit die on the cross also, as one God? Of course, the Church teaches that only Jesus, God the Son, was crucified. I do not believe that panentheism could lead to such confusion. Keep it a mystery.

At the beginning of the fourth century C.E. a priest and theologian named Arius (died 336) became very popular. His theology focused more on the humanity of Jesus. Arius insisted that God the Father had existed before God the Son. Arius taught that God the Son was inferior to God the Father. He stated that God the Son did not exist eternally with the Father, but was created by the Father as an instrument for the creation of the world. God the Son was considered to be a lesser deity. He was not fully and eternally God from

189

before all time. In describing the relationship between God the Father and God the Son, Arius wanted to use the Greek term *homoiouson*, meaning that God the Son, (Jesus,) was "like" or of "similar" substance with the Father, but "not of the same substance" with the Father. The Greek word *homoousion* means "equal to, identical with, or the exact same."[50] The difference in spelling of the two Greek words in question is one iota. But, that distinction caused a huge division throughout the Christian world, even to the point of igniting riots and violence. Another similar theory called "Adoptionism" stated that Jesus was not the eternal Son of God, but that God the Father adopted him as his "Son" sometime after Jesus was born, perhaps at Jesus's baptism, when Jesus supposedly heard God say, "You are my Son, by beloved; my favor rests on you." ("St. Luke" 3:22.) These were taken to be denials of Jesus's eternal divinity, equal to God the Father. Other bishops and theologians declared that they were heretical. The Christian Church was polarized and in an uproar! These divisions became dangerous. I view them as mythological. Did Jesus exist eternally, from before all time, as the Nicene Creed and the Creed of Athanasius state? No one knows. It is a theological theory. But, for most Christians today, it is best left as a mystery. No one is about to go to war over those issues as in the past. (I hope.)

The Emperor of the Holy Roman Empire, Constantine, wanted to use Christianity as a force to unite his empire. Constantine recently had accepted Christianity as his religion, and therefore as the religion of the empire. Not long before that time, Christians had been persecuted. This was a radical change. In his wisdom, Constantine realized that the Christian faith was becoming more and more popular. A brilliant political move was to say, "If you can't beat them, join them." Now, Christianity was to be the common faith, the glue that united the empire and held it together. All the dissention and divisions over theological issues, however, had threatened to divide, rather than unite the empire. Constantine had to find a way to establish unity and peace. He did this by calling together a council of bishops and theologians from all around the empire. This was to determine what was "the Mind of the Church," that being, what was to be the true, orthodox, universally accepted faith, and what was unacceptable as heresy. It was believed that the Holy Spirit would guide the council toward truth.

The first general council met at Nicaea in Asia Minor in 325. About 318 bishops attended. The leader was St. Athanasius. The council declared that Arianism and similar theories which resembled Adoptionism were heretical. The equal relationship between God the Father and God the Son was expressed by the Greek word *homoousion*. This meant that God the Son was of one and the same substance as God the Father, eternally existent with the Father, and equal to the Father. *Homoiosion* was rejected. To us today, this all may seem ridiculous. For me, this shows the folly of trying to define God so precisely. In the year 325, however, it was of extreme importance, both to the Christian Church and to the Empire. (Tragically, religion never can be separated from politics.) These definitions are reflected in the creeds. The Nicene Creed states that Jesus Christ is "the only Son of God, eternally begotten of the Father, God from God, Light from Light, true God from true God, begotten, not made, of one being (substance) with the Father." [51] The Nicene Creed in the present Roman Catholic liturgy states that Jesus is "consubstantial" (*homoousion*) with the Father. Is Jesus like God or the same as God? No one knows. To me, it is not important. I know Jesus mystically. I consider the theological details to be mysteries. I believe that this illustrates why most Quakers, historically and currently, emphasize mystical, direct revelation over scripture, creeds and doctrines.

Theodore (350-428,) Bishop of Mopsuestia, put emphasis on the humanity of Jesus. This emphasis was common among the theologians of Antioch. He taught that Jesus Christ was in every way a human being, a man, with a human person and also a human nature. Theodore believed that Jesus was united to God from the moment of his conception, but their relationship was like any relationship between humans. The union was only a matter of degree. This reduced Jesus to being merely a good man. It denied that he is God himself acting through human nature. This Christology, also called "Nestorianism," taught that the man Jesus was a distinct person from God the Son. Official Church doctrine teaches that Jesus Christ is one person, God the Son, acting through two distinct natures, human and divine. [52]

In opposition to the emphasis put on the humanity of Jesus among the theologians in Antioch, some in Alexandria swung again to the opposite interpretation, believing that Jesus had no real human nature. When God became a man, they stated, the divine and human natures were mixed to form one divine-human nature. This belief was called "Monophysitism." [53]

The various councils of the early Church defined very specifically what was "orthodox" or "Catholic," meaning what was to be believed according to the "Mind of the Church" as expressed by the gathering of bishops and theologians. They clearly defined what was heretical. Throughout its entire history, the Christian Church has been challenged by heresies. I agree with Arius, Nestorius, Pelagius, Abelard and many more heretics. (*Mea culpa!*) That does not bother me. Most are irrelevant in terms of panentheism. These historical heresies are the results of attempts to define mysteries in human terms. I have spent much of my adult life teaching traditional, systematic theology. That led me to rejecting much of it. Bishop James Pike once said that since he did not believe the creeds literally, he preferred chanting them rather than reciting them. They simply are symbolic hymns of a past era. Theorize no more! (Should I be burned on a stake?)

I cannot help but to think of the tragic attempts that have been used to enforce Christian doctrines. A glimpse at the history of Europe alone is dominated by wars. Usually these have been about leaders, rulers, land, natural resources, politics and wealth, but the battle cries too often are religious. Theological doctrines are merely insufficient human theories. Understanding each other is more important than understanding Church doctrines. Animosity still exists between "liberals" and "conservatives." Much of it is related to politics. Christians remain divided.

The Resurrection

On previous pages, I have described my theory of the Atonement, and offered reasons why I reject the traditional beliefs that Jesus was offered on a cross as a blood sacrifice to God to pay for the sins (original and actual) of mankind. I view that as mythology, and also as an unfortunate image of an angry God needing to be appeased. Now, I shall consider theories of Jesus's post-crucifixion appearances.

Something following Jesus's crucifixion was tremendous, extreme, radical and revolutionary enough to change his followers from total despair into ecstatic joy. It evoked faith so strong that they would live and die for it. We call this "The Resurrection." How it happened, we do not know. The point is, something huge happened!

After many of the followers of Jesus had experienced the risen Christ, they responded to that miracle with such glorious enthusiasm, that they wanted to tell everyone that Jesus had defeated death, and indeed, was alive. Those who experienced the living Jesus after his death, however, told very different stories about their experiences. He was not recognized immediately by many. For some, he was a spirit who walked through locked doors. For others, he was very physical, with scars from the wounds on his body. He was hungry and ate. For others, he was known in breaking bread at supper, and then he disappeared. It is because of these different accounts that I believe that the experiences that many had of the living Jesus after his crucifixion were mystical appearances. He was not a resuscitated corpse. No one knows what happened to Jesus's corpse. It may have been placed in the tomb owned by Joseph of Arimathea, as scripture claims. It may have been moved and placed elsewhere. It may have been buried in a mass grave, which was the usual method of disposing the bodies of those who had been crucified. The Jewish customs regarding the celebration of Passover complicated matters. Many different theories abound among theologians. That does not mean that Jesus's appearances after his death were not real. They were very real, but they were experienced through a different consciousness from normal, human perceptions. He did defeat death. Jesus Christ is alive today. The accounts that we read in scripture are the results of those responses on the parts of those who originally experienced Jesus alive after his crucifixion. To those people, the experiences actually happened. But, the only way that later writers could express their overwhelming enthusiasm, was through legends and exaggerations. Yes! There was "fire" before there were the legends. Today, we use those legends of scripture to try to find the fires that created them, the sources that ignited the fires that eventually led through the legends to faith.

I do not use the word "resurrection" in the same way that it has been used by most Christians throughout the ages. Traditionally, it has been believed that Jesus's physical body was raised from the dead three days after his crucifixion. "Three" is a magic number for Hebrews. Actually, it was believed by some that the "soul" hovered around a dead body for four days, and then moved on elsewhere. If Jesus had been crucified on a Friday just before dusk, Saturday at sundown would have been one day. Supposedly, he was resurrected on Sunday morning. That was not three days. What is most important, however, is to understand that something earth shaking, shocking, unexpected, overwhelming and miraculous must have been experienced. It remains a mystery.

Theologians usually do not say that "Jesus arose from the dead." Instead, they emphasize that this was an act of God. Most prefer to say that "Jesus was raised from death." God raised Jesus from death. This was beyond human power, which to me, means that it must be seen in terms of the

197

numinous, through the experiences of mysticism. It is a divine mystery that cannot be explained in human terms. That enhances my belief that the appearances of Jesus were mystical, not of the physical consciousness associated with our normal perceptions. They were not responses to a resuscitated corpse. But, for those who experienced them, they were real. Mystically, they are real!

Consider the many conflicting accounts of Jesus appearing to various people after his crucifixion. In "St. Luke" 24:13ff., we read that Jesus suddenly appeared to two men who were walking from Jerusalem to Emmaus. At first the men did not recognize Jesus, even though they had known him well before his crucifixion. Then, after Jesus had joined them for supper, and broke bread with them, they recognized him. Suddenly, Jesus disappeared.

In "St. John" 20:17, Mary Magdalen came to Jesus's tomb, weeping. Two angels appeared where Jesus's body had been. Then suddenly someone else appeared to her. She thought that it was the gardener. Then, only after he spoke to her did she recognize Jesus. He said to Mary, "Do not cling to me, because I have not yet ascended to the Father." ("St. John" was written about 110 C.E.)

In "St. John" 20:19-31, there is a story of Jesus walking through locked doors to join his apostles at a meal. Here he seems to be a spirit. Yet, he showed them the wounds on his hands and his side. When confronted later by Thomas, who doubted that it was Jesus, Thomas was told to put his finger in Jesus's wounds. Here, within the same story, we see Jesus first as a spirit coming through locked doors, and then as a physical, resuscitated corpse. In "St. Luke" 24:36-42, in what seems to be the same story, Jesus appears again to his apostles, saying, "Look at my hands and my feet; yes, it is I indeed. Touch me, and see for yourselves; a ghost has no flesh and bones as you see I have." Then he asked for something to eat, and he ate some grilled fish. Because of these, and other discrepancies in the various accounts of Jesus's appearances, I conclude that these must have been subjective, mystical or spiritual experiences. That does not, however, make them less real. It says that they were experienced through a consciousness in the realm of the numinous, rather than in the human realm that we associate with perceiving physical bodies.

In his "First Letter to the Corinthians" St. Paul wrote what is considered the earliest known written account of resurrection experiences. Paul wrote, "...Christ died for our sins, in accordance with the scriptures." (What scriptures? Paul wrote this letter around 57 C.E., before any of the four gospels were written.) Paul continued, "...that he (Jesus) was raised to life on the third day..., that he appeared first to Cephas (Peter) and secondly to the twelve. Next, he appeared to more than five hundred of the brothers at the same time, most of whom are still alive, though some have died; then he appeared to James and then to all the apostles, and last of all he appeared to me too; it was as though I was born when no one expected it." ("First Corinthians" 15:4-8. Jerusalem Bible.) This all is very strange, because Paul's conversion to Christianity did not happen until decades after Jesus's so-called "Ascension." By that time the Church had been established in many areas. ("Acts" 9:1-19.)

For me, this is extremely important, because Paul's conversion is considered to be the same kind of "resurrection" experience as were those that occurred shortly after Jesus's crucifixion, and certainly before his alleged ascension. For me, that means that the experiences that the followers of Jesus had of his living presence with them was not limited to the time that he supposedly was on the earth before his "ascension into heaven."

The authors of the gospels believed that above the earth, somewhere in the far-off sky, there was a place called "heaven" where God dwelt. They seem to have believed that the appearances of Jesus after his death were somehow in physical, human bodily form, although this was confusing to them. After people ceased to experience the resurrected Jesus present with them, the writers of "St. Matthew" and "St. Luke" felt that they had to explain what had happened to Jesus. Where was he? Why did he not appear again? Therefore, they invented the story of Jesus's ascension into heaven. (See "St. Mark" 16:20, "St. Luke" 24:51.) For those of us who do not believe that Jesus had appeared as a physical, resuscitated corpse, that is not an issue. Most Christians, historically, have believed that the resurrected Jesus was a resuscitated corpse raised from the dead. What does all of this mean as we think of Jesus alive with us today? It says for me, that Jesus appeared to his followers, and continues to appear to us, in a "glorified body," not a resuscitated corpse. When we speak of the "resurrection of the body," we do not mean our physical, earthly bodies. We mean a glorified body which no one can describe, but which each person "sees" in a variety of personal, subjective ways, through a mystical lens in the realm of the numinous. [54] Jesus continues to appear to us.

In "First Corinthians," St. Paul wrote what he believed about Jesus's resurrected and glorified body, and his hope for our lives after physical death. This makes it very clear to me that Paul did not believe that Jesus's physical corpse was resuscitated into life and had appeared as such to his followers. St. Paul described the resurrection of Christ as a "glorified body," which appeared to him decades after Jesus's crucifixion. In "First Corinthians" 15: 35-53. Paul wrote:

> Someone may ask, 'How are dead people raised, and what sort of body do they have when they come back?' They are stupid questions. Whatever you sow in the ground has to die before it is given new life, and the thing that you sow is not what is going to come back. You sow a bare grain, say of wheat or something like that, and then God gives it the sort of body that he has chosen; each sort of seed gets its own sort of body.... There are heavenly bodies and there are earthly bodies; but heavenly bodies have a beauty of their own and earthly bodies a different one.... It is the same with the resurrection of the dead. The thing that is sown is perishable; but what is raised is imperishable. The thing that is sown is contemptable, but what is raised is glorious. The thing that is sown is weak, but what is raised is powerful. When it is sown, it embodies the soul, when it is

202

raised it embodies the spirit. If the soul has its own embodiment, so does the spirit have its own embodiment.... As the earthly man (Adam) was, so we are on earth; and as the heavenly man is, so we are in heaven. And we who have been modeled on the earthly man, will be modeled on the heavenly man. Or else, brothers, put it this way, flesh and blood cannot inherit the kingdom of God, and the perishable cannot inherit what lasts forever.... We are not going to die. We shall be changed..., because our present perishable nature must put on imperishability, and this mortal nature must put on immortality. When the perishable nature has put on imperishability, and when this mortal nature has put on immortality, then the words of scripture will come true: 'Death is swallowed up in victory....' so let us thank God for giving us the victory through our Lord Jesus Christ. (Jerusalem Bible.)

For me, these words of St. Paul explain the resurrection of Jesus, and our eternal existence also. Taking them one step farther, for me, they mean that the appearances of Jesus are continuous events. Ever since Paul's experience of the living Christ on the Damascus Road, countless others throughout the ages have been confronted by the living Jesus in much the same ways. These experiences are real. They are not illusions or mere visions. Jesus is their source. They begin with him, not with the persons who experience him. They are divinely inspired, not just humanly imagined. If that were not so, how can one explain the complete changes in the attitudes of the apostles and followers of Jesus from absolute despair at the crucifixion, to suddenly becoming overwhelmingly joyful after somehow encountering Jesus alive? How can one comprehend the devotions of thousands of saints who have given their lives for Christ? This did not happen merely from reading in the <u>Bible</u> about a man who had lived centuries before. It had to have been something much more profound and personal, something that radically changed their lives, so that they devoted their entire existence, even to death, as a response to experiencing the living Jesus. This had to have been a mystical experience of the living presence of Jesus through mystical, direct revelation.

Most clergy, other than fundamentalist, have studied Biblical criticism. Many are afraid that if they tell congregations that many of the accounts in scripture are legends, they will destroy people's faith. To perpetuate belief that these legends are historically true, however, leads others to conclude that Christianity is based on a lot of "fairy tales." Mysticism is the answer!

Life After Death

I believe that God is eternal and that God is love. If God loves us personally and individually, as most Christians believe, then would God cease to love us when we cease to function in our mortal bodies? God is within each of us. Since God is immortal, therefore, we must be immortal also.

The Christian Church has proclaimed throughout the ages that after death, there is a resurrection of the body. But, that body is to be considered a "glorified body." Born in 1937, I certainly do not want to spend an eternity with my present, worn-out, old body, bad knees, wrinkles, aches and pains. I plan to have my corpse reduced to ashes. Some say that an eternal "soul" leaves the body at death. The separation between body and soul is a Greek idea. That is not convincing to me. The creeds state the resurrection of a "body."

We may try to imagine what our glorified bodies will look like. That is a mystery. I do not know what will happen to me after my death. I try to believe that because God lives eternally within me, I too shall live eternally. That is a matter of faith and hope. Is it reasonable?

Do I have doubts about life after death? Most certainly. Most of us would like the comfort of believing in a life after death. We all have a desire for immortality. It is comforting to believe in a heaven or paradise, where we could be reunited with those whom we have loved on earth. What a joy it would be if I could believe that someday I could meet Jesus and the saints. I would be so anxious to be reunited with my parents, grand-parents, aunts, uncles and scores of friends who have died. What a pleasure it would be to greet my ancestors, about whom I have done so much genealogical research! In a parish discussion on the afterlife, one elderly woman asked how all the myriads of people who ever have lived possibly could fit into heaven. Another asked how she would be able to find her parents and her husband among all those people. Then a third widow confessed that she hoped that her husband never would find her. I did not want to attack their faith by arguing that heaven is not a "place." I wish that I had the comfort of that naïve faith. Was paradise invented just to give gullible mortals that comfort?

It is very difficult to believe something if our reason tells us that it is not true. Faith, however, can go beyond reason. Whether eternal life is a comforting hoax or reasonable hope, I try to believe that something wonderful awaits me in the future. That is a comforting hope, which I have clung to in spite of many doubts. Again, who knows? A prayer for the dead from the 1979 Episcopal Book of Common Prayer, states: "...that increasing in knowledge and love of Thee, they (the departed) may go from strength to strength in thy heavenly kingdom." [55] Do I believe in a judgment? No. Those concepts were created by men to keep society in order, and to even out the injustices of this life. Do I accept Roman Catholic beliefs about purgatory? Absolutely not. Purgatory was a ridiculous, tragic attempt to control life after death by the Catholic Church, and thereby to make money. Life after death is a dimension which we cannot begin to fathom. Eternal life cannot be thought of in terms of "places." I believe that hell is a human invention. We all have hopes and fears.

In the gospels, the idea of eternal life is described in the present tense. It can become the condition of our lives at any moment. Eternal life, therefore, is a condition that does not begin or cease when our bodies die physically. Life transcends both time and physical death.

God has been experienced as a power of love within us and yet beyond us. If God loves us personally and individually, as Christians believe, then would God cease to love us when we cease to function in our mortal bodies? Because God loves us eternally, we must live eternally as the objects of God's eternal and absolute love. Jesus's resurrection, and ours, are not about resurrected corpses. They are about God's eternal love, and therefore, our eternal existence. We are part of that divine existence. The human and the divine are one "Existence." For me, this makes the inevitability of death easier to accept. It is compatible with my sense of reason. Can faith transcend reason? Faith is mystical. Reason is cerebral.

Usually, within my meditations, I remember each of my departed, close relatives and many friends. Often, I feel a mystical bond with them. Then, I focus on Jesus, and await communication from the Spirit. For me, this is real. I cling to a belief that Jesus overcame death, and exists in a "glorified body" that we all may imagine in our own subjective ways. In spite of doubts, I try to maintain a hope that in some way I shall continue to exist eternally as an object of God's eternal love. As far as I am concerned, nothing more can be said. No one has returned from a future life. It is all right to have faith and doubts at the same time.

Moral Theology:
How Do We Know What Is Right?

Love God, and do as you please.
St. Augustine of Hippo.

During my three years at The Episcopal Theological School in Cambridge, Massachusetts, I had taken a number of courses in moral theology and Christian ethics. My professor was Dr. Joseph Fletcher, known as "the father of situation ethics." His teachings and books have been condemned by Roman Catholics. My professor at Saint Augustine's College in Canterbury, England, Bishop John A.T. Robinson, taught much the same philosophy. (See J. A. T. Robinson, Honest to God.)

Roman Catholic official doctrines state, and most Protestant fundamentalists believe that every act has an intrinsic value of virtue or evil built into its very definition. They believe decisions about the good or evil, right or wrong of any act are dictated by an authority such as scripture or the Church. This is called "essentialistic moral theology." Laws which define right or wrong are upheld regardless of the situation. Each specific act is always good or evil, therefore, as stated by the authority which defines it. One cannot commit an evil act in order for a good act to result. The end cannot justify the means. For example, one cannot rob the rich (stealing is an evil act) to help the poor, or to save one from starvation. One cannot abort a fetus to save the life of a mother who has a severe heart condition and probably would not survive childbirth. (There are exceptions to this under the rules of the Double Effect and casuistry. These require complex, legalistic definitions and precedents which are not necessary for this discussion.) A priest cannot break the confidentiality of the confessional in order to save an innocent man's life. One cannot lie about where a person is hiding in order to save that person from harm. Numerous examples can be considered.

Situation ethics, on the other hand, state that there are no intrinsic values in any particular act in and of itself. Each act must be judged as right or wrong according to the situation. There are no universally good or evil acts. The same act may be right in one situation, but wrong under different conditions. As opposed to essentialistic moral theology, the end must justify the means. Murder, for instance, may be the right thing to do in certain severe situations such as the abortion of a hopelessly diseased fetus, or withholding nourishment, medicines or life-support devices from a terminally ill person, war or self-defense. (This is different from casuistry, which is an authoritarian legal system based on precedents.) Honoring one's parents may not be a good act if the parents are abusing a child. Stealing from a wealthy person may be justified to avoid starvation if one is absolutely destitute. Lying may be the right thing to do if a priest denies knowing about an incident that was told to him under the seal of the confessional. In situation ethics, the only authority is one's personal, individual conscience. One's conscience must judge every act according to its unique situation in terms of selfless Christian love, called by the Greek word, *agape*. Selfless love is the most important concept of situation ethics. *Agape* means love that expects nothing in return. It may demand sacrifice and suffering. It is pure love for the sake of others. Jesus's life is the perfect example of *agape*.

In essentialistic moral theology, our conscience becomes the "policeman" that tells us whether or not we are obeying a prescribed law. Those laws must have been defined by an authority beyond the individual. The faithful must learn them and abide by them. The conscience, therefore, must be conditioned, programmed or informed about the laws defining good or evil acts. For the situationalist, however, each individual's conscience is the "judge" or decision maker, which decides what is right or wrong in each particular situation, based on selfless love. We always must be aware of who programs our consciences. Consciences are programmed by our cultures and experiences. That is not the same as direct revelation, which is divinely inspired.

In "First Corinthians" 6:12, St. Paul wrote, "All things are lawful for me, but not all things are helpful." In chapter three, verses 23-27 of his "Epistle to the Galatians," St. Paul wrote, "Christ redeemed us from the curse of the law.... Before faith, we were allowed no freedom by the law.... The law was to be our guardian until Christ came and we could be justified by faith." I believe that *agape* must challenge and often supersede laws.

Opponents of essentialistic moral theology claim that it is an arbitrary legalistic system. No law can apply to every situation. Certainly, no act can be discovered to be consistently right or wrong universally, in every land, religion or culture. That disregards the individual and the specific circumstances surrounding any act. Also, who has the authority to tell everyone what is right or wrong in all situations? In civil cases, there are laws with juries and judges to interpret them. That is a different story.

Opponents of situational ethics will argue that all humans are capable of rationalizing any act to convince themselves and others that it is permissible. Any subjective decision could be rationalized to justify anything, leading to social chaos, anarchy and confusion. (I raise the question, "Would it have been justified to assassinate Adolf Hitler?") Such individual freedom is too much to expect of sinful humanity. Mankind must be ruled by absolute laws and controlled by authorities. In the heat of blind anger, I might decide that it would be acceptable for me to harm or even kill someone who really has hurt me, or threatened my safety. Overwhelmed with passion I might want to touch a woman inappropriately. We all could take the law into our own hands by becoming vigilantes. Perhaps we need laws to keep us from acting in irrational, highly emotional states. (Read Dostoyevsky's novel <u>The Brothers Karamazov,</u> "The Grand Inquisitor." Compare it to Thomas Hobbes's <u>Leviathan</u>. A fascinating debate.)

Of course, most people use a combination of legalism and situation ethics. Most everyone will try to abide by the rules of those who hold authority over them. Those laws may be accepted freely, as in the cases of Christian denominations which a person may or may not join. Or they may be laws of the land imposed by civil authorities.

213

When it seems impossible to abide by those rules, people may act against them as their conscience advises them.

Many Roman Catholic priests today approach moral problems from a pastoral point of view, respecting the laws, but also considering the circumstances. Love and mercy finally seem to be taking precedence over strict, authoritarian legalism. This often becomes obvious in cases of artificial contraception. Most priests who personally cannot justify the prohibition against artificial contraception are addressing questions about it individually and pastorally with their parishioners. One priest recently told me that contraception was the hot issue during the past decades. Today the hot items are abortion and gay marriage. Every generation focuses on some specific moral issue. Remember the temperance debates among Protestants at the turn of the last century that led to Prohibition? What a mess!

When I taught courses in Moral Theology at a Roman Catholic university, my classes would discuss the pros and cons of each approach. After much discussion on both sides, I instructed the classes on various issues, such as papal infallibility, Biblical literalism versus critical analysis, the primary and secondary justifications for sexual relations, the ban against artificial birth control, abortion, a patient's right to die without medical intervention, euthanasia, capital punishment, the absolute seal of the confessional, immigration, homosexuality, celibacy, cloning, stem cell research, race relations, a just war, conscientious objection, our involvement in various foreign conflicts, international disarmament, the right to protest, ecology, the protection of nature and so on. Each student had to write a research paper, at least twenty-five typed pages on a subject of his or her choice. (This was before the days of computers!) There were scores, perhaps over a hundred topics from which students could choose. Everyone in my classes was questioning the issues we discussed. Debates were exciting! Much of my teaching was during the 1960s and 1970s, when everything was being questioned. It was a fascinating era. Never stop questioning!

(Teaching in Roman Catholic institutions was a unique experience for me as a liberal Episcopal priest. It could have happened only during those ecumenical years, 1963-1975. Then came a reactionary backlash. Today, a papal mandate states that teachers of religion must be Roman Catholics and approved by their bishops. It was great while it lasted! I continued to teach at other, secular colleges.)

Why Be Good?

At the Catholic preparatory school where I was teaching, one day I caught two boys cheating in a major test in my humanities class. That class involved a lot of history, making it necessary for the students to memorize names, events and dates. I quietly called the boys to my office after the test. They admitted that they had "ponies" with events and dates on them, and that they had cheated. I failed them on their tests, but not for the semester. Then we had a long talk. After having experienced four years at a Quaker college (Haverford) under its unique and excellent honor system, cheating was not a temptation or even a consideration. I had grown accustomed to trusting others never to cheat as well. We often took exams in our rooms, but we never would cheat or refer to our books.

In our class discussions about cheating, it took a while for many of my students to break out of the mentality that anything is all right if one does not get caught. Some of the boys believed that if you do not get caught doing something wrong in this life, you will pay for it in the next life. The virtuous will be rewarded for their good works. Evil deeds will incur punishment. That is how justice is achieved. Many doubted it. Most agreed with the theory that perhaps heaven and hell are humanly devised mechanisms invented to keep societies in order and to give people a sense of justice, if not in this world then in the next.

I maintained that moral conduct cannot be based on desire for reward or fear of punishment in this life or beyond death. Morality must be based upon personal integrity, respect for others and for oneself. For some, this was a novel idea.

There is a story that I often used in sermons about a nun who was walking down a road carrying a bucket of holy water. She met a monk along the road who was carrying a censer filled with red hot coals. The nun said that with the holy water she was going to quench the fires of hell, and the monk said that with those coals he was going to burn down the palaces of heaven, so that people would do the right, moral thing without fear of punishment or desire for reward. They would be motivated only by their love for God and for the people around them. Eventually the boys got the idea, after they broke through years of indoctrination that morality was motivated by punishment or rewards. Something now had to be considered that many had not thought about before. It is called "integrity," love of God, neighbor and self. If we could achieve that, then no laws would be necessary. After much class discussion, one of my students responded to it all saying, "You must realize, Father, that honesty is not going to get me into college. I think that the only way to get ahead in this world is to be smart enough to avoid getting caught." Maybe Dostoyevsky's Grand Inquisitor was correct. I hope not! But, no society can exist without enforceable laws. What is the answer?

Serious Decisions: Prayer

What do moral theology and ethical decision making have to do with mysticism and direct revelation? They offer good examples of what this book is about in terms of everyday life.

The differences between situation ethics and authoritarian, legalistic moral theology reflects the differences between mystical, direct revelation on one side, and the authorities of literalistic interpretations of scripture or of a codified, doctrinal system on the other. In situation ethics, scripture may serve as a guide, but it is not to be the absolute rule for making decisions about morality. Fundamentalists take scripture literally. Roman Catholic are expected to obey codes of virtues and vices. Of course, most fundamentalists and Roman Catholics pick and choose what laws they want to follow, and what they disregard. We all do that. But, one system demands obedience to an authority above the individual. The other places the responsibility of decision making upon the individual's personal, subjective decisions in the context of any situation or set of circumstances. What is right in one case may wrong in another. No action has an intrinsic value built into it.

Reason plays the largest part in making most decisions based on situation ethics. Reason is based on a thought process that is within normal human consciousness. It is our everyday mechanism for making decisions. We consider all the facts. We try to think logically. We try to anticipate all the possible repercussions of our decisions. We often ask the utilitarian question proposed by John Stuart Mill, "What will bring the best possible outcome to satisfy the greatest number of people?"

I am proposing a different, more profound process of making decisions, especially when those decisions will have momentous repercussions on ourselves and on others. I am thinking of such issues as abortion, removing life support from a terminally ill patient, divorcing one's spouse, volunteering for military service, accusing a family member of a crime, or resigning from a job. I could go on and on with examples. When these decisions confront us, many Christians will turn to prayer and meditation. We search for answers beyond our own abilities to reason without rationalizing or to debate logically, and to make the right choices.

In terms of situation ethics, I would propose that through meditation, we enter the realm of direct revelation. Some will say that it is the Holy Spirit speaking to each person. I agree. But the Holy Spirit has to be recognized in a realm beyond human perceptions. In order for us to know what is right or wrong directly from beyond ourselves or any authority, we can try to enter a realm of the supernatural, the realm of the numinous. This is what much of prayer is all about. For the situationalist, one's conscience can be informed through direct revelation from God. This is found in the realm of the sacred, the supernatural, the numinous. We reach that realm through the process of prayer and profound meditation. I call that that process "mystical."

In the words of Rufus M. Jones: **"Wherever in the universe the good is being achieved, wherever truth is triumphing, wherever holiness is making its power known, there is Spirit, there is God."**

(Religious Foundations. Palala Press, *Internet.* 2016. p.11.)

Summary

I have struggled with the Christian faith throughout my adult life, and searched through many diffcrent denominations. Finally, I concluded that the accounts of scripture are, for the most part, legends, parables, myths and hyperbole. Christian doctrines and creeds assume an obsolete and false concept of the universe. They presume to define God in intricate, mythological, human terminology, as a divine super-human dwelling in a celestial "place" called "heaven." Scripture and doctrine can provide guidelines and contexts for faith. They may offer us inspiration, but they never can be taken literally or historically.

As a non-theist Christian. I do not believe that God is a divine "person" or supreme "being." We can, however, experience God in many ways. "Panentheism" is an expression of God as "God-in-All." God is in every person, in all that exists and yet is greater than existence itself. God may be said to be "Existence" itself.
(Read Bishop John Shelby Spong's books!)

For me, the most compatible expressions of my faith are found among The Religious Society of Friends, the Quakers. One of the most basic foundations of Quakerism is mysticism. Through mysticism, one can reach a level of consciousness which is beyond, and more profound than our normal human modes of thinking and perceiving. This is called "the sacred realm of the numinous."

Quakers believe that there is a "Light" or presence of God in every person. This is called the "Inner Light." Therefore, we need to try to see God in every person, and treat every person as we would want to be treated, or as we would treat a loved one. That becomes our moral obligation. When we do not live up to our God-given potentials to be loving people, that is called "sin," or *hamartia*. In Greek, h*amartia* means that we fail to hit or rise to our targets, meaning our potential best, our highest ideals. God's Inner Light always is within each of us, and in all others. Therefore, we are not a fallen, basically evil humanity, as orthodox Christianity teaches. If God is the "Ground" of every person's being, and the divine Inner Light is present in every person, then our essence is not evil. Jesus was not sacrificed to appease an angry God for the sins of an evil humanity. Jesus shows us that God is Love. Through God's power within us, we can temper our propensity toward sin and evil, and strive to rise above it to our ideals, our divinely inspired potentials. Jesus shows us the way.

God does not direct the events of our lives. As mortals, we live with limitations, accidents, aging, illnesses and eventually death. Prayer does not influence God to intervene in our lives, but prayer enables us to experience God within ourselves, in all persons, and in every aspect of life. Through prayer we can influence our own lives, and the world around us. Prayer is mystical. Prayer transmits energy. Love is prayer in action.

I reject traditional Christian doctrines and creeds which "dissect" Jesus Christ as they have attempted to define how he is both human and divine. I find those attempts to be unnecessary and misleading. Jesus is the full, perfect and unique manifestation (human image) of God. Jesus and God are One. That says it all. God is alive within every person. God is in ALL. God is Existence.

Christianity in its "mainstream" form must be completely reinterpreted and differently communicated. Can this ever happen? How? Liturgies, sermons and public prayers all express obsolete interpretations of the Christian faith that I reject. So where does one turn for insight and guidance about the Christian religion? For many Christians, scripture and doctrines fail. Where then can one find identity in worship and beliefs? Do not lose hope. God is alive within each of us.

Pray and meditate. Discover another level of consciousness. The sacred, mystical realm of the numinous can carry you to God. Look within yourself. You will meet Jesus personally. You will experience God! You will find strength to accept, forgive and love. You will find serenity.

Many years ago, while I was serving as a priest in a large parish, I was experiencing a difficult time, theologically and personally. I asked a bishop, who also was a good friend, if, with all of my doubts and heretical beliefs, I should leave the priesthood and find some other occupation. The bishop told me that my faith was as valid as that of any other Christian. It simply was experienced and expressed differently. He told me to keep studying, questioning and searching. A critical knowledge of scripture and theology can be interesting academically, said the bishop, but it also can challenge orthodox faith. I call it the curse of a questioning mind.

Recently, I have returned to my early family experiences and education among Quakers. Most of my theological theories are consistent with those of traditional Quakerism. My "liberal" political tenets are based on my Quaker beliefs. With many Quakers, I reject religious boundaries. God is All, within All, and beyond All! **PEACE.**

Mentors Who Greatly Influenced Me

I have been influenced most by the Rt. Rev'd. John Shelby Spong, the Episcopal Bishop of Newark, New Jersey. Also, I rely on my former teacher, Bishop John A.T. Robinson of Woolwich, England, the Most Rev'd. Frank T. Griswold, the Rt. Rev'd. Robert DeWitt, the Rt. Rev'd. Paul Moore and other Episcopal bishops. I have studied books by Hans Kung, Jacques Maritan, Karl Rahner, Bernard Haring, Edward Schillebeeckx, Pierre Teilhard de Chardin, Yves Conger, Rosemary Ruether and Charles Curran, (many of whom later were condemned by popes as heretical.) I rely on the writings of Joseph Campbell, John Dominic Crossan, N.T. Wright, Bruce Chilton, Marcus Borg and other members of the "Jesus Seminar." (I have read 15 books written by Bishop John S. Spong, and 7 by Marcus J. Borg, both members of the Jesus Seminar.) Also, I have studied publications from the Society of Friends at Pendle Hill, Wallingford, Pennsylvania, and other Quakers including Rufus Jones, my former teacher Douglas Steere, Elton Trueblood, Robert Barclay, Thomas D. Hamm, Leonard Kenworthy, Andrew Harvey, Pink Dandelion and Wilmer Cooper. In the field of Moral Theology, the subject that I mainly taught, I follow my seminary professor, Dr. Joseph Fletcher.

End Notes

1. Spong, John Shelby, <u>Jesus for the Non-religious</u>. HarperSanFrancisco. 2007. p. 133.

2. Otto, Rudolf, <u>The Idea of the Holy</u>. 1923. P.C. Almond. J.W. Harvey, Trans. 1974.

3. Woods, Richard, O.P., <u>Understanding Mysticism</u>. Iimage Books. Doubleday & Co. NY. 1980. p. 20.

4. *Ibid.*

5. *Ibid.*, p. 21.

6. Dandelion, Pink, <u>An Introduction to Quakerism</u>. Cambridge Press, Cambridge. 2007. p.120.

7. Youngblut, John, "Speaking As One Friend to Another." Pendle Hill Pamphlet # 249. Pendle Hill. Wallingford, PA. 1983. p.15.

8. *Ibid.*, p. 12.

9. *Ibid.*, p. 17.

10 Dandelion, *op.cit.* p.136.

11. Otto, Rudolf, The <u>Idea of the Holy</u>. P.C. Almond, Trans. 1974.

12. Cozzens, Donald, <u>Sacred Silence</u>. "Denial and Crisis in the Church." The Liturgical Press. Collegeville, Minn. 1997. p.159.

13. <u>Sacramentum Mundi</u>, "An Encyclopedia of Theology." Karl Rahner, Ed. Herder and Herder, NY. 1968. Vo. 2. p. 274.

14. Campbell, Joseph, "A Dialogue Between Joseph Campbell and Bill Moyers. "The Power of Myths." Internet. billmoyers.com/series/joseph-campbell-and-the-power-of-myth. PBS Series. June 21, 1988.

15. Spong, John Shelby, <u>Eternal Life</u>: "A New Vision." HarperOne, NY 2009. p. 146 ff.

16. Robinson, John A.T., <u>Honest to God</u>. The Westminster Press. Phila., PA. 1963. p. 22.

17. "Process Theology." Internet. <u>http://theopedia</u>. com/process/theology. (9-22-2016.)

18. Spong. *op. cit.*, <u>Eternal Life</u>. pp. 121-124.

19. Spong. *Ibid.* 152.

20. Robinson, *op. cit.* p. 22.

21. *Ibid.* p. 46.

22. *Ibid.*

23. <u>Oxford Dictionary of the Christian Church</u>. F.L. Cross, Ed. Oxford University Press. NY. 1958. "Logos."

24. Braden, Gregg, <u>The God Code</u>. Hay house, Inc. California. 2004. "Einstein."

25. De Chardin, Pierre Teilhard, S.J. Internet. "Pierre Teilhard deChardin." http//www. ignatianspirituality.com/gnatian-voices-20th - century-voices/pierre-teilhard de-chardin-sj.

26. *Ibid.*, "Hymn to the Universe."

27. Youngblut, *op. cit.* p. 15.

28. *Ibid.*, p. 22.

29. Robinson, *op. cit.* p. 76.

30. Macort, John G., <u>A Reasonable Covenant</u>. Audubon Press. New Haven, CT. 1995. pp. 180-181.

31. Borg, Marcus, <u>Jesus</u>. HarperOne. 1989. p. 31.

32. Spong, John Shelby, <u>The Sins of Scripture</u>. HarperSanFrancisco. CA. 2005.

33. <u>Oxford Dictionary of the Christian Church</u>. *op. cit.* "Immaculate Conception."

34. *Ibid.* "Assumption of the B.V. Mary."

35. Spong, *op. cit.* <u>Jesus for the Non-religious</u>. p.133.

36. Spong, *op. cit.* <u>Eternal Life</u>. p. 167.

37. *Ibid.*

38. Dandelion, *op. cit.* p.136.

39. <u>Oxford Dictionary of the Christian Church</u>. *op. cit.* "Incarnation." p. 684.

40. Robinson. *op. cit.* p. 67.

41. *Ibid.* p. 66.

42. *Ibid.*

43. *Ibid.* p. 71.

44. Spong. *op. cit.* <u>Eternal Life</u>. p. 167.

45. Lewis, C.S., <u>Essay Collection</u>: "Faith, Christianity and the Church. HarperCollons. London 2000. p. 141.

46. Spong. op. cit.. <u>Eternal Life</u>. p. 168.

47. Spencer, Bonnell, O.H.C., <u>Ye Are the Body</u>. Holy Cross Press. West Park, NY. 1961. p. 72.

48. *Ibid.*

49 *Ibid.*

50. Spencer, *op. cit.* p. 81.

51. The Book of Common Prayer. The Episcopal Church. 1976. "The Creed of St. Athanasius." pp. 864-865.

52. Spencer, *op. cit.* p. 106.

53. Oxford Dictionary of the Christian Church. op. cit. "Monophysitism."

54. Spong, *op.cit.* Eternal Life. pp. 176-182. and Borg, *op. cit.* Jesus, p. 289.

55. Book of Common Prayer. *op. cit.* p. 481.

BIBLIOGRAPHY

Armstrong, Karen, <u>A History of God</u>. Ballantine Books. NY. 1994.

Borg, Marcus J., <u>Jesus,</u> "Uncovering the Life, Teachings and Relevance of a Religious Revolutionary." HarperOne. NY. 2006.

Borg, Marcus, Editor, <u>Jesus and Buddha</u>. Ulysses Press. Berkeley, CA. 1997.

Braden, Gregg, <u>The God Code</u>. Hay House, Inc. California. 2004.

Buber, Martin, <u>Ecstatic Confessions</u>. "The Heart of Mysticism." Harper and Row. NY. English translation, 1985.

Buber, Martin, <u>Ecstatic Confessions</u>, "The Heart of Mysticism." Esther Cameron, Trans. Harper and Row. San Francisco. 1985

Bullfinch, Thomas, <u>Mythology</u>. Spring Books, London, 1964.

Butler, <u>Butler's Lives of the Saints</u>. Concise Edition. Michael Walsh, Ed. Harper and Row. San Francisco. 1956.

Campbell, Joseph, <u>Myths to Live By</u>. Bantam Books, NY. 1977.

Chilton, Bruce, <u>Rabbi Jesus</u>. "An Intimate Biography." Image Books. Doubleday, NY. 2000.

Cooper, Wilmer A., <u>A Living Faith</u>, "A Historical and Comparative Study of Quaker Beliefs." Friends United Press. Richmond, Indiana. 2001.

Cox, Harvey, <u>The Future of Faith</u>. Harper-Collins. NY. 2009

Cozzens, Donald, <u>Sacred Silence</u>, "Denial and the Crisis in the Church." The Liturgical Press. Collegeville, Minn. 1997.

Crossan, John Dominic, <u>Jesus</u>, "A Revolutionary." Harper-San Francisco. 1944.

Dandelion, Pink. <u>An Introduction to Quakerism</u>. Cambridge University Press. 2007.

Ehrman, Bart D., <u>Did Jesus Exist?</u> HarperOne, NY. 2012.

Ehrman, Bart D., <u>Jesus Interpreted</u>, "Revelations in Hidden Contradictions in the Bible." HarperOne. NY. 2009.

Fletcher, Joseph, <u>Situation Ethics</u>. John Knox Press. Westminster. 1966.

Gray, John, <u>Near Eastern Mythology</u>. Hamlyn Publishing Group, Ltd. London. 1969.

Gomes, Peter J., <u>The Good Book</u>. William Morrow and Co., Inc. NY. 1996.

Griswold, Frank T., <u>I Have Called You Friends</u>. Cowley Publications, Cambridge, MA. 2006.

Harkins, James Gibson, (Pseudonym for John G. Macort.) <u>The Curse of a Questioning Mind</u>. Createspace, Charleston, SC. 2011.

Hamilton, Edith, <u>Mythology</u>. Signet. NY. 1940.

Jones, Rufus M., <u>Religious Foundations</u>, Internet. Palala Press. Rufus M. Jones. 2016.

Kelsey, Morton T., <u>Myth, History and Faith</u>. "The Remythologizing of Christianity," Paulist Press. NY. 1974.

Kenworthy, Leonard S., <u>Quakerism</u>, "A Study Guide on the Religious Society of Friends." Quaker Pub., Kennett Square, PA 1983.

Kvekerforlaget, <u>Quakerism, a Way of Life</u>. In Homage to Sigrid Helliesen Lund. Norwegian Quaker Press. Oslo, Norway. 1882.

Loconte, Joseph, <u>The Searchers</u>. Thomas Nelson. Nashville. 2010.

Mennenger, Karl, <u>Whatever Became of Sin?</u> Hawthorne Books. NY. 1973.

Mack, Burton L, <u>The Lost Gospel</u>, "The Book of Q and Christian Origins." Harper San-Francisco. 1993.

Macort, John G., <u>A Reasonable Covenant</u>. "Rational Approaches to Christian Theology" Audubon Press. New Haven, CT. 1995.

Moyers, Bill, <u>Healing and the Mind</u>. Doubleday, NY. 1995.

<u>Oxford Dictionary of the Christian Church</u>. F.L. Cross, Ed. Oxford University Press. NY. 1958.

Nolan, Albert, <u>Jesus Before Christianity</u>. Orbis Books, Maryknoll, NY. 2001.

Otto, Rudolf, <u>The Idea of the Holy</u>. 1923. P.C. Almond. J.W. Harvey, Trans. 1974.

Rahner, Karl, "Concerns for the Church, Theological Studies XX." Trans. Edward Quinn. Crossroads, NY. 1998.

Robinson, John A.T., <u>Honest to God</u>. The Westminster Press. Philadelphia. 1963.

Rubenstein, Richard E., <u>When Jesus Became God</u>. A Harvest Book, Harcourt, Inc. NY. 1999.

<u>Sacramentum Mundi</u>, An Encyclopedia of Theology." Karl Rahner, Ed. Herder and Herder, NY. 1968. Vols. 1,2, 4 and 5.

Spencer, Bonnell, O.H.C., <u>Ye Are the Body</u>. Holy Cross Press. West Park, NY. 1961.

Spong, John Shelby, <u>Eternal Life</u>: "A New Vision." HarperOne. NY. 2009.

Spong, John Shelby, <u>Living in Sin</u>, "A Bishop Rethinks Human Sexuality."Harper and Row. San Francisco. 1988.

Spong, John Shelby<u>, Rescuing the Bible from Fundamentalism</u>. HarperSanFrancisco. 1991

Spong, John Shelby, <u>The Sins of Scripture</u>. HarperSanFrancisco. 2005.

Spong, John Shelby, <u>Why Christianity Must Change or Die</u>. "A Bishop Speaks to Believers in Exile." HarperSanFrancisco. 1998.

Spong, John Shelby, <u>Jesus for the Non-Religious</u>. HarperCollins, NY. 2007.

Other books read in the past by Bishop Spong: <u>Honest Prayer</u>, <u>The Hebrew Lord</u>, <u>Liberating the Gospels</u>, <u>Resurrection, Myth or Reality?</u>

Whitmire, Catherine, <u>Plain Living</u>, "A Quaker Path to Simplicity." Sorin Books, Notre Dame, IN. 2001.

Woods, Richard, O.P., <u>Understanding Mysticism</u>. Image Books. Doubleday & Co. Garden City, NY. 1980

Yungblut, John, "Speaking as One Friend to Another." Pendle Hill Pamphlet #249, Pendle Hill. Wallingford, PA. 1983.

Notes

Made in the USA
Middletown, DE
06 May 2018